Pract

Kl

1993

Hayit Publishing

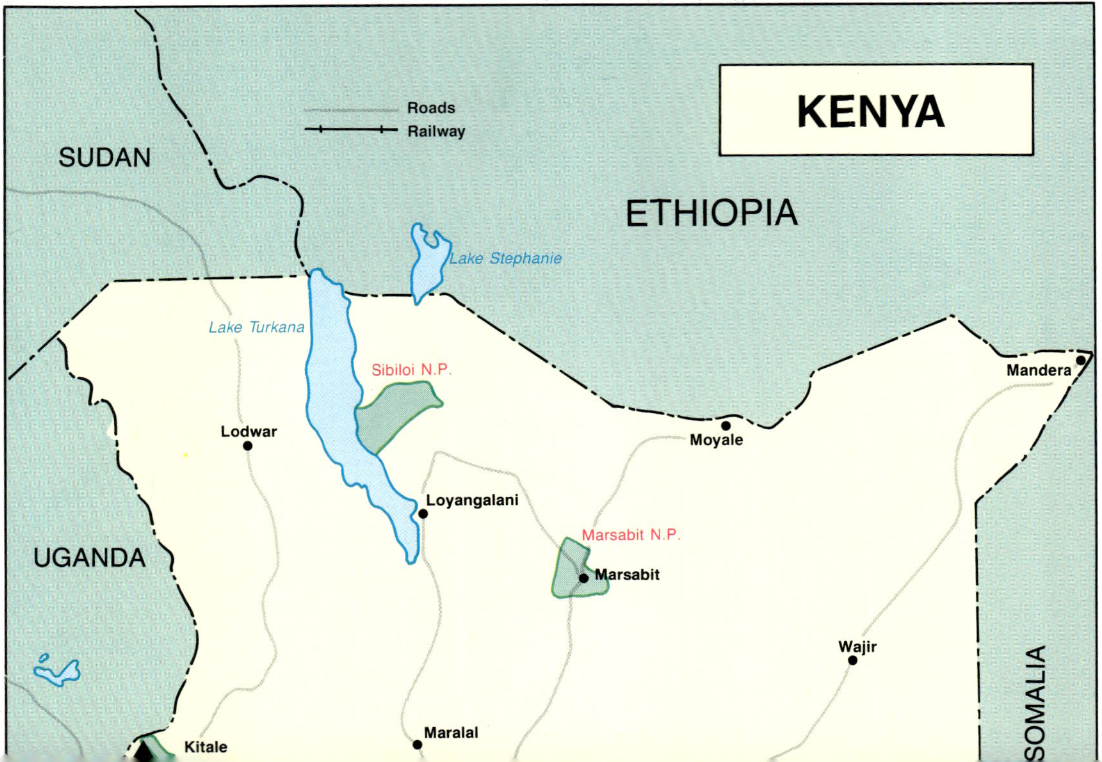
KENYA
Roads
Railway
SUDAN
ETHIOPIA
Lake Stephanie
Lake Turkana
Sibiloi N.P.
Mandera
Lodwar
Moyale
Loyangalani
Marsabit N.P.
Marsabit
UGANDA
Wajir
SOMALIA
Maralal
Kitale

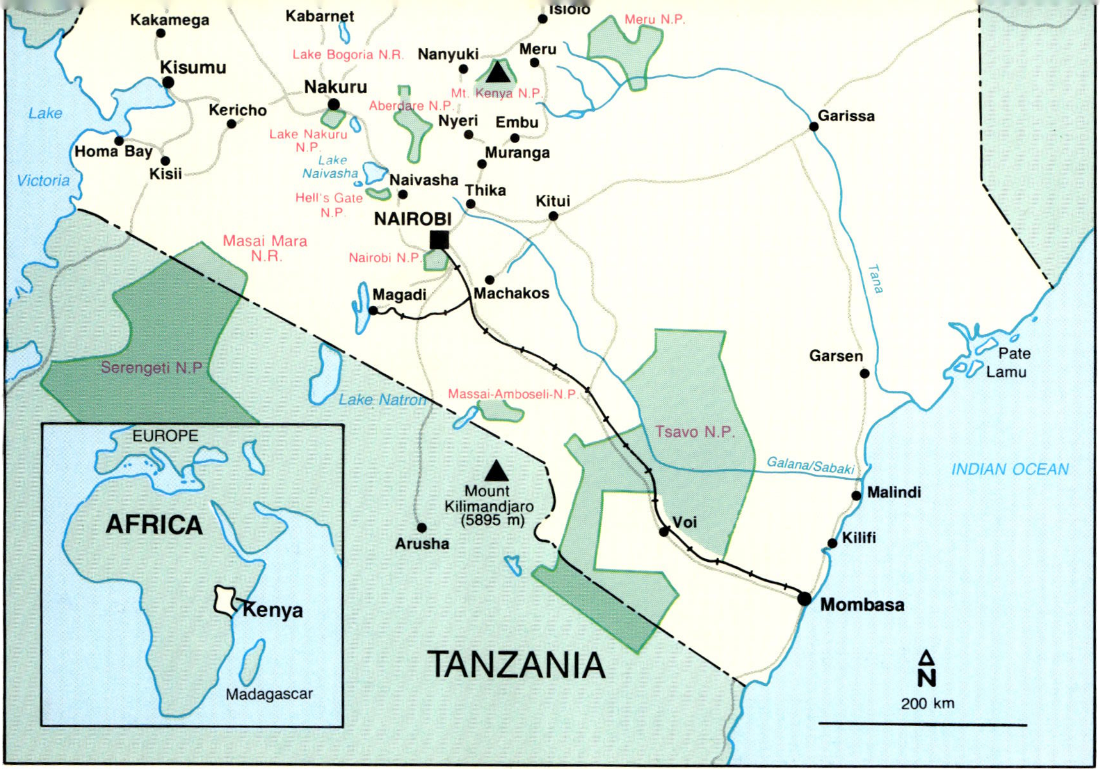

Kakamega
Kabarnet
Isiolo
Meru N.P.
Lake Bogoria N.R.
Nanyuki
Meru
Kisumu
Nakuru
Mt. Kenya N.P.
Lake
Kericho
Aberdare N.P.
Nyeri
Embu
Garissa
Lake Nakuru N.P.
Homa Bay
Muranga
Kisii
Lake Naivasha
Naivasha
Victoria
Thika
Hell's Gate N.P.
Kitui
NAIROBI
Masai Mara N.R.
Nairobi N.P.
Tana
Magadi
Machakos
Pate
Lamu
Garsen
Serengeti N.P
Lake Natron
Massai-Amboseli-N.P.
Tsavo N.P.
EUROPE
Galana/Sabaki
INDIAN OCEAN
Mount Kilimandjaro (5895 m)
Malindi
AFRICA
Voi
Arusha
Kilifi
Kenya
Mombasa
TANZANIA
N
200 km
Madagascar

1st Edition 1993
UK Edition: ISBN 1 874251 03 7
US Edition: ISBN 1 56634 013 6

Author: Ole Helmhausen
Translation: Birgitt Schippers
Adaption, Revision: Scott Reznik
Print: Scholma Druk, Bedum, NL
Photography: Ole Helmhausen

 Printed in the Netherlands

Contents

Registry of Places

General Information

Using this Book

Books in the *Practical Travel* series offer a wealth of practical information. You will find the most important tips for your travels conveniently arranged in alphabetical order. Cross-references aid in orientation so that even entries which are not covered in depth, for instance ''Holiday Apartments,'' lead you to the appropriate entry, in this case ''Accommodation.'' Also thematically altered entries are also cross-referenced. For example under the heading ''Medication,'' there appear the following references: ''Medical Care,'' ''Pharmacies,'' ''Vaccinations.''
With travel guides from the *Practical Travel* series the information is already available before you depart on your trip. Thus, you are already familiar with necessary travel documents and maps, even customs regulations. Travel within the country is made easier through comprehensive presentation of public transportation, car rentals in addition to the practical tips ranging from medical assistance to newspapers available in the country. The descriptions of cities are arranged alphabetically as well and include the most important facts about the particular city, its history and a summary of significant sights. In addition, these entries include a wealth of practical tips — from shopping, restaurants and accommodation to important local addresses. Background information does not come up short either. You will find interesting information about the people and their culture as well as the regional geography, history and current political and economic situation.
As a particular service to our readers, *Practical Travel* includes prices in hard currencies so that they might gain a more accurate impression of prices even in countries with high rates of inflation. Most prices quoted in this book have been converted to US$ and £.

Aberdare National Park

Located in the Aberdare Mountains, this park covers an area of 767 square kilometres (296 square miles) and extends from Nyahururu in the north to Nairobi in the south. The highest peaks are Ol Doinyo Lesatima (4,001 metres/12,005 feet in altitude) in the north and the Kinangop (3,909 metres/11,730 feet). The vegetation is unique: although the equater is close by, this region is surprisingly reminiscent of Scotland with a landscape of heather, clear mountain streams and moors veiled in wafts of mist during the morning hours. Its picturesques vistas of waterfalls, impenetrable bamboo forests (which Mau-Mau guerrillas used as a hiding place in the 1950's) and alpine vegetation growing up to a height of 6 metres (20 feet) make up this region of the park, rarely visited by tourists. A large diversity of wildlife (lions, leopards, hyenas, reed bucks, duikers, buffaloes, elephants and occasionally rhinoceroses) are especially common in the western area of the park where the mountain slopes descend more gently. Because of the park's average altitude of 3,000 metres (9,810 feet) above sea level, nights can be severely cold with temperatures dropping below the freezing point.

Note: If travelling by car, the park roads are only passable during good weather. The park entrances are near →*Nyeri,* Mweiga and along the road to Naivasha.

Accommodation: Kiandongoro Fishing Lodge, inexpensive accommodation with self-catering units along the Magura River, centrally located within the park.

Accommodation

In Kenya, travellers can choose from a number of different types of accommodation — everyone will certainly find a place to stay the night. In Nairobi and Mombasa as well as in the larger cities of the country, there are hotels which meet international standards; it is certainly not surprising that the highest priced accommodations are in the two largest cities. The price level starts at £16.70 ($31.25) for a double room including breakfast at places which mainly accommodate tourists. At the beach hotels and in the luxury lodges of the national parks and game reserves, one must pay the highest prices. It is also possible to pitch one's tent everywhere after asking permission. Hotels managed by Kenyans are noticeably less expensive while offering the same level of service. ''Boarding & Lodging'' is an accommodation category below the hotels. ''B & L's'' can be found in every city and small village. They are sparcely furnished, but surprisingly clean, safe and inexpensive. One will certainly also notice the ''hoteli.'' Different to what the name might suggest, this is not a hotel where one can spend the night but only a bar also serving snacks.

Prices quoted in this guide are listed as follows £XXX (single room)/£XXX(double room) and the respective dollar prices in brackets. They are meant to serve only as an orientation and cannot be exact due to changes in the exchange rate.

Air Travel →*Travelling to Kenya, Travel in Kenya/By Air*

Amboseli National Park

This park lies almost a two hours by car south of Nairobi at the foot of Mount Kilimandjaro (5,845 metres/19,113 feet). Pictures of wild animals taken against this unique backdrop of the snow covered Kilimandjaro, the highest mountain in Africa, are known throughout the world. The Uhuru Peak can best be seen during the morning and evening hours. Where once Earnest Hemingway was inspired to write his famous stories by the untouched wilderness, the park's ecosystem, covering an area of 3,200 square kilometres (1,235 square miles), is dangerously threatened by safari tourism. Nevertheless, the park still offers sufficient living space for many types of animals: lions, elephants, cheetahs, leopards and several kinds of antelope are especially predominant in the areas surrounding the Enkongo Narok and Olkenya swamps. The small herd of rhinoceroses has seemed to have once again recovered from the unchecked poaching. 420 distinct species of birds live in the acacia woods in the park's bushlands as well as in the swamps fed by runoff from Mount Kilimandjaro.

Accommodation

Ol Tukai Lodge (for reservations contact: Nomads Kenya Ltd., P.O. Box 24793, Nairobi, Tel: 331826). Inexpensive, self-catering huts are located centrally in the park. There is also a general store and places for campfires.

Amboseli Lodge, c/o P.O. Box 30139, Nairobi, Tel: 723776, £57/£72 ($108/$135).

Kilimandjaro Safari Lodge, c/o P.O. Box 30139, Nairobi, Tel: 337510/27136, £55/£71 ($104/$133).

Amboseli Serena Lodge, c/o P.O. Box 48690, Nairobi, Tel: 339800, £50/£62 ($94/$117). Much quieter in comparison to the lodges listed above.

A self-catering camping area can be found south of the Amboseli Serena Lodge outside of the park.

Automobile Club

The Automobile Association (AA) in Kenya is located in Nairobi. Its address is: Hurlingham (shopping centre), P.O. Box 40087, Nairobi, Tel: 720382. The AA also helps in planning one's own travel route, provides information on the road condi-

tions and can recommend car rental agencies. Those who become a temporary member of the AA will receive a list of the nationwide network of automobile repair services.
→*Emergencies*

Bargaining

It is almost good manners to bargain with prices. In the sphere of tourism, native car rental agencies, taxi drivers and the owners of hotels agree on prices from time to time, especially during off-season *(→Tourist Season).* One should remain objective and not irritate the other party with exaggerated expectations. Those who go shopping in the markets and at the stands along the roads can be sure they will be taken advantage of — even when they were able to talk the price down by a fantastic 50%!
Since the prices for food are very low, this loss can easily be absorbed. In the supermarkets and the Asian shops, all prices are labelled and bargaining is inappropriate as is the case in all restaurants.

Beaches

White beaches shimmer between coconut palms and cassowary trees, below the cloudless blue sky and embedded in an exotic Arabian-African environment: reality almost always lives up to what the colourful prospects promise at home. Kenya's coast is the centre of the tourism in East Africa and is especially attractive because of its proximity to world-famous game reserves such as the →*Tsavo National Park* and the →*Amboseli National Park* at the foot of Mount Kilimandjaro.
A paradise? Not entirely! The negative effects of tourism should not be underestimated. The fact that time and again new hotel grounds displace entire villages, that the traditional arts and crafts have become increasingly tacky, and that the complacent behaviour of many tourists, aggravated by the bad economical situation, makes it difficult for many Kenyans to maintain their dignity. These comments are not intended to spoil one's trip, but they should open some eyes to the reality of a paradise with some flaws.
Mombasa divides the coast into two different sections. An increasing number of tourists spend their holidays on the beaches south of the city because they are longer and wider than the beaches in the north and, therefore, not so quickly crowded. Coral reefs some hundreds of miles off the northern as well the southern coast make a natural barrier warding off algae, and above all barracudas and sharks so that one can enjoy water sports. During low tide it is possible to walk out to

the reef. However, one should wear plastic sandals during this hike since not only stranded coral lie in the water holes, waiting for the next flow tide but also sea urchins, which one can inadvertantly step on and whose spines may cause a bad infection.

The beaches south of Mombasa are accesssible by a ferry to the mainland. The most popular bathing areas are Likoni located directly beyond the mooring, and Diana, 22 miles further to the south. The hotels listed below are mostly booked as part of a package tour. These offer the entire range of tourist services which can be also used by people, who are not guests of the hotels.

Likoni: Shelley Beach Hotel, P.O. Box 96030 Mombasa, Tel: 451001/2/3/4, £9.35/£15 ($17.50/$28.15). This surprisingly inexpensive, well-kept beach hotel located about 3 kilometres (2 miles) from the Likoni ferry.

Diani: Africana Sea Lodge, P.O. Box 84616 Mombasa, Tel: 0127-2624 Diani, £25.70/£38 ($48.15/$71.25).

Jadini Beach Hotel, P.O. Box 84616 Mombasa, Tel: 0127-2622 Diana, £27.70/£41($51.90/$76.90).

Diani Reef Grand Hotel, P.O. Box 35 Ukunda, Tel: 0127-2723/2195 Diani, £50/£79 ($92.50/$147).

Golden Beach Hotel, P.O. Box 31 Ukunda, Tel: 0127-2625 Diani, £33/£45 ($60/$85).

Leisure Lodge Hotel & Club, P.O. Box 84383 Mombasa, Tel: 0127-2620/2012, £35/£47 ($66/$88) and £53/£71 ($99/$132) for club rooms. This is definitely the finset address on the coast.

Leopard Beach Hotel, P.O. Box 34 Ukunda, Tel: 0127-2110/2111/2113/2721 Diani, £73/£40 ($46/$72).

Nomad Beach Bandas, P.O. Box 1 Ukunda, Tel: 0127-2155 Diani, £13/£21 ($24/$39). Self-catering; located in a lovely beefwood grove.

Robinson Baobab, P.O. Box 32 Ukunda, Tel:0127-2026/7/8 Diani, £42/£70 ($80/$132).

Safari Beach Hotel, P.O. Box 90960 Mombasa, Tel: 0127-2726/2131/2088 Diani, £32/£42 ($60/$80).

Tradewinds Hotel, P.O. Box 8 Ukunda, Tel: 0127-2016/2116 Diani, £32/£41 ($59/$77).

Two Fishes, P.O. Box 23 Ukunda, Tel: 0127-2101/2/3 Diani, £33/£43 ($61/$80).

All hotels offer considerable discounts during low season *(→Tourist Season).*

Restaurants: Each of the hotels listed above house at least two good and up to three very good restaurants under their palm thatched roofs. Those who want to

Broad, white beaches await holiday visitors, not only along the coast at Diani ▶

forego the meals offered in the hotels, will soon make dining out their favourite evening passtime. For many years, the Ali Barbour's (Tel: 2033 Diani) located in a coral cavern has had an especially good reputation. This exclusive restaurant serves French cuisine and exquisite seafood. Relatively new are the Galaxy Chinese Restaurant (01261-2529/2291 Diani), and the Indian Restaurant Maharani, which is in a little fairy-tale castle like something out of Arabian Nights. If one decides to visit one of these restaurants, one should ask the hotel reception to organise transportation. Never walk to these restaurants — unfortunately, tourists have already been attacked along the streets.

Freetime Activities: Of course, there are many ways to spend the days pleasantly. Those who are "tired of relaxing" and have had enough of all the water activities can join one of the numerous safaris organised by the hotels. Among the most popular are trips to the →*Tsavo National Park* lasting several days. Twin-engine aircrafts even take visitors to the Masai Mara Game Reserve which is 1,000 kilometres (650 miles) from the coast. The flight alone passing the snow-covered Mount Kilimandjaro is worth the trip. One can also rent a car, for example at Glory Car Hire in the modern shopping centre of Diani, or a bicycle perhaps?

To reach the beaches north of Mombasa, one exits the city, crossing the Nyali Bridge. The beautiful beaches of Nyali, Bamburi, Shanzu and Kikambala line the coast like a string of pearls.

Nyali: Mombasa Beach Hotel, P.O. Box 90414 Mombasa, Tel: 471861, £36/£47 ($66/$88).

Reef Hotel, P.O. Box 82234 Mombasa, Tel: 471771/772/775/776 and 472448/472777, £27/£39 ($50/$73).

Bamburi: Neptune Beach Hotel, P.O. Box 83125 Mombasa, Tel: 485701/3, £12/£29 ($21/37).

Severin Sea Lodge, P.O. Box Mombasa, Tel: 485001/05, £37/£52 ($69/$97).

Traveller's Beach Hotel, P.O. Box 87649 Mombasa, Tel: 485121-6, £26/£29 ($49/$56).

Whitesands Hotel, P.O. Box 90173 Mombasa, Tel: 485927/8/9, £33/£51 ($62/$94).

Shanzu: Hotel Intercontinental, P.O. Box 83492 Mombasa, Tel: 485811/5, £47.37/£65.70 ($88.75/$123.15). Best hotel north of Mombasa.

Serena Beach Hotel, P.O. Box 90352 Mombasa, Tel: 485721/2/3/4.

Kikambala: Whispering Palms Hotel, P.O. Box 5 Kikambala, Tel: 374/5/6, £30/£40 ($57/$75).

Beverages →*Cuisine*

Buses →*Travel in Kenya*

Camping

Tenting in Kenya holds a special fascination. Sleeping under the stars by a campfire provides the opportunity to experience the African wilderness firsthand as well as leaving unforgettable impressions. In the national parks, most of the campsites are very simple (sometimes, the only way these can be recognised is by a sign reading ''campsite''), but are located in an idyllic landscape and are very inexpensive. Camping in the cities on youth hostel or hotel property is also possible in many cases.

Camping off of campsites requires that permission be asked. This type of camping is, in contrast to other countries, relatively safe in Kenya — provided, of course, one does not provoke wild animals. One should by no means pitch a tent in a dry riverbed or on a path used by big game.

→*individual entries*

Car Rental

Travellers will find every type of vehicle imaginable in Kenya. Compared to public transportation, renting a car offers much more mobility and the invaluable advantage of being able to plan visits to the national parks. Buses and taxis are not allowed to enter the parks.

The following is required when renting a car:

The driver must be at least 23 years of age and must present a valid driving licence, issued at least two years prior.

All of the main offices for rental car agencies are located in Nairobi or Mombasa. Since the competition is stiff, one is well advised to bargain with the price. Discounts and special rates are available both during the →*tourist season* and the low season. Note: quite often the more expensive jeep models are recommended although four-wheel drive may not be necessary. The AA will be helpful in recommending the appropriate vehicle for a given tour.

The local car rental agencies are much less expensive than the international companies like Avis and Hertz and are no less reliable. Some of these rent out jeeps complete with camping equipment *(→Nairobi).*

The average prices as an orientation: a Fiat Uno costs about £9 ($17) plus £5 ($9.50) per day. About 10p (20 cents) are charged for each kilometre driven. When a rental contract is signed, a deposit or credit card is required.

Addresses: →*Nairobi, Mombasa*

→*Travel in Kenya*

Central Island National Park

Central Island is located in the middle of Lake Turkana and was declared a national park and nature reserve only a few years ago. Removed from the stream of tourists, it is one of the very special sites in Kenya. The island, with an area of only 5 square kilometres (1.95 square miles), is an extinct volcano with three dark, grey-black peaks towering to the sky, which can be seen when approaching by boat. The crater lakes are hidden beyond the forboding shore. These lakes are the habitat of an enormous colony of aquatic birds. However, the main attraction of the island is its crocodile population. The rugged shores lining the crater lakes count among the continent's largest breeding grounds for crocodiles. During the months of April and May, hundreds of crocodile offspring hatch from their eggs.

The Lake Turkana Fishing Lodge (P.O. Box 509, Kitale) on Ferguson's Gulf organises boat tours to Central Island National Park.

Chale Island

The untouched beauty of this island, measuring only 600 metres (1,962 feet) in length and the marvellous sandy beach falling gradually off into the sea, characterise the pristine attraction of this island, far removed from the tourist beaches. This island is located south of Diani Beach *(→Beaches).* The beach hotels of Diani Beach organise day tours including beer and a barbecue (Africana Sea Lodge and Two Fishes among others).

Cheques *→Money*

Climate

One of the biggest attractions of Kenya is its climate. Majestic mountain chains, extensive highlands and gigantic inland lakes have such an influence on the air currents that all in all the weather is drier and cooler, and the landscape of the country is not as wooded as in the other countries of Equatorial Africa. While in the other parts of the tropical belt, the clashing trade winds provide for heavy rainfall twice a year, Kenya comprises many different climatic zones and vegetation, allowing for travel even in the middle of the rainy season without any problem (*→Tourist Season).*

Unique vegetation, magnificent shows of nature and diverse wildlife make a visit to Aberdare National Park an unforgettable experience ▶

In the highlands, the climate is remeniscent of Central European weather. During the hottest season (January to March) it is seldom warmer than 28 °C (82.4 °F), while it can cool down to 14 °C (57.2 °F) at night. During the tropical winter (June to August) the temperatures may even reach a low of 5 °C (41 °F). The respective temperatures for Mombasa are higher: the average temperatures average 32 °C (87.8 °F) between January and March, and fall to ''arctic lows'' of 24 °C (75.2 °F) at night. During the winter, the temperatures are slightly lower.

Clothing and Equipment

Without question, different equipment is necessary for a holiday at the beach in Malindi than is required for estensive hikes in the Mount Kenya region. For those who forgot to pack one or the other article necessary for hiking the mountainous regions or an extensive tour through the entire country, specialised equipment shops in Nairobi help fill this gap. The following stores can be recommended:
''Colpro,'' Kimathi Street
''Bella Boutique,'' Kenyatta Avenue
''Adelphi,'' Kaunda Street
''The Spin and Weave Shop,'' Kimathi Street
''Woolworth,'' Kenyatta Avenue, corner of Kimathi Street (across from the New Stanley Hotel).
Visitors who plan on travelling around the country should be prepared for all types of weather — almost every type of weather occurs in Kenya. The basic equipment and clothing needed, consists of light cotton shirts and loosely fitting trousers or skirts. A stable pair of jeans are appropriate for the relatively cool highlands. It is also advisable to bring along two sweatshirts. Wool clothing is indispensable for mountain tours and safaris. For hikes on Mount Kenya and Mount Elgon, angora underwear, down jackets, mittens, hiking boots, rain gear and possibly climbing gear should also be packed. Whether on the coast, in the mountains or in the desert, a hat and a light neck scarf are a must since the sun in this equatorial region is so intense that severe sunburn could otherwise result.
Footwear: a pair of sturdy shoes, a pair of sandals and a pair of plastic sandals for the beach. Tennis or jogging shoes will prove appropriate in the cooler regions, but are not suited for the coast and northern Kenya.
Although a tuxedo is not mandatory in the international restaurants of Nairobi and Mombasa, it is customary to dress appropriately: men should wear long trousers (shorts should be worn only on the beach!); women should not wear tight-fitting trousers; knee-length skirts are more suitable. What can be considered a minimum

for Nairobi is even more strict in Moslem dominated coastal regions. Unfortunately, many visitors disregard this.

One suitcase or shoulder bag will be absolutely sufficient for a holiday on the beach. For those who wish to see more of the country, it is recommended to bring along not only a large backpack but a day-pack as well. When using a hotel as a base for a safari, articles which are not needed on the trip should be left in the hotel and that which is brought along should be carried in a day-pack — travelling light in the literal sense.

Photographic equipment is best carried in a padded aluminium case as can often be seen in Kenya. Opportunity breeds thieves: an old, ragged bag is just as functional and does not draw undue attention.

Other convenient articles to bring along are:

Plastic bags for laundry and to protect against dust, toilet paper, a travel alarm clock, ear plugs, a sewing kit, a pocket knife with a bottle and can opener, candles and a pocket lamp.

Conduct → *Culture*

Credit Cards

''Plastic'' as an alternative to cash or traveller's cheques has become increasingly popular in Kenya during the last few years. In the meantime Euro Card, American Express and VISA are accepted by all tourist facilities without any problems. One can use credit cards in hotels and restaurants or when shopping. A special advantage of these cards is: if paying for a flight or rental car by credit card, one is automatically insured. Thus, it is useful to get information on the service and contractual conditions of the various credit card companies before departure. One will also be informed of the names of representatives as well as of the places in Kenya where cash can be withdrawn from a credit card account.

Crime

Kenya is — what is usually forgotten in the posh of the luxury tourist hotels — a classic third world country. The differences in wages are enormous, the majority of the population lives in absolute poverty. Thus, it is not surprising that criminal offences against tourists have recently increased. *(→Theft).*

After dark, one has to be aware that armed robberies do take place, especially in Nairobi. It is advisable to take a taxi if the destination within the city is further away *(→Nairobi).* Yet, towns off the tourist track and in the rural areas are more safe than they appear at first sight. Some routes in the northeastern regions of Kenya (for example Isiolo — Marsabit) and between Amboseli and Tsavo West are only driven in convoy — those who have a rental car should not tempt fate, but join such a convoy. In general, the best way to avoid possible hazards is through prevention: be sure not to flaunt prosperity, not to handle money carelessly, to keep all valuables under lock and key, and to avoid, as much as possible, crowds and other chaotic situations. Never trust a stranger when exploring Kenya's night life, and always keep a cool head.

Cuisine

The long history of Kenya is reflected in the diversity of its cuisine. With the arrival of the Arabs, Indians, Portuguese, English, and finally the tourists, the traditional millet, fruit and roots were augmented with further ingredients. The coconut tree came from the Indo-Pacific region to East Africa; sugar-cane, rice and mango fruit came from Asia; the Portuguese imported cotton, maize, cassavas, pineapples,

Brilliant colours of the traditional costumes and jewellry are characteristic of the Samburu, whose tribal name means "butterfly" in English

peanuts, cashews, avocados and papayas from Brazil. The English brought along coffee, tea as well as their eating habits and times (''five o'clock tea''). With the influx of tourists and the worldwide popularity of the American way of life, hamburgers and french fries were also introduced.

Africa is not a paradise for gourmets. The meals are simple, but nourishing and tasty. They are not only prepared in private kitchens but also served in the inexpensive ''hotelis'' *(→Restaurants).* ''Ugali,'' a white or yellow paste made from corn is a typical Kenyan dish, served with or without fish. ''Irio'' is a thick paste made from beans, corn and potatoes. ''Matokeist'' is a puree of cooking bananas, and a popular side dish served with chicken and mutton. ''Wali na nyama'' is rice with meat, ''wali na maharagwe'' consists of rice with brown beans. ''Nyama ya kuchoma'' means grilled meat, ''nyama ya ng'ombe '' and ''nyama ya mbuzi'' are rice with beef and goat respectively. Note: ''kuku'' means chicken, and grilled chicken is served in all possible (and impossible) variations. Of Indian origin are the ''chapatis,'' simple pancakes made from flour and water and used to dip.

Often confusing: one cannot stay the night in the local hotelis, but one can enjoy the food and drink

''Curry'' means a thin, spicy sauce, as well as a dish which is seasoned with it (''curries''). However, ''Masala tandoori'' is a heavy, rich sauce. ''Biriani,'' a rice dish with vegetables and chicken, is especially popular in the coastal regions. Rice is served with ''kebabs'' (meat roasted on a spit), ''mushkaki'' (marinated pieces of meat) and ''kema'' (minced meat). ''Pilau'' is a standard dish consisting of spiced rice with vegetables. Tourists especially like all of the dishes baked in coconut milk, for example ''kuku paka'' (chicken in coconut milk).
Snacks include ''samosasa,'' triangular puffed pastries fried in oil and filled with meat or vegetables. Also available on the streets are ''kutumbuo,'' baked rice bread, and ''kwini keki,'' little pieces of cake in the shape of a crown (''kwini'' is equivalent to the English ''queen''). The dishes mentioned above may not suit everyone's taste, but Kenyan fruit has a good reputation everywhere. The enormous variety of fruit ranges from pineapples and papayas, to coconuts, bananas, mangoes and delicious citrus and passion fruits. Sweet tea and beer are the Kenyan's favourite beverages. The most widely known kinds of beer are Tusker, White Cap and Pilsner. Other alcoholic beverages are Kenya Cane (white rum) and Kenya Gold, a golden-coloured coffee liqueur. Produced in Kenya since 1983, the papaya wine is available as a white or a rosé wine and is absolutely recommandable as a table wine. Soft drinks such as Cola, Fanta, Seven-Up etc. are sold all over the country, as are mineral water and fruit juices.

Culture

To speak of one culture is an impossiblity when considering the 42 ethnic groups and almost as many different languages and dialects existing in Kenya today. The colonial period and Christianisation have ultimately turned the old tribal societies upside down. Nevertheless, the daily life of the Kenyans has still been strongly characterised by traditional values since a decisive break from the traditions never occurred. Farmers as well as city people, shoe cleaners as well as governmental employees still follow the generally binding basic values. One of these is most certainly common to all peoples of Kenya: the precedence of interrelationships over individualism, which is considered asocial.

Religion

Kenyans are a deeply religious people. This is not rooted in missionary work or the Islam, but in the pre-European period, when religious concepts and the afterlife pervaded every aspect of daily life. The concept of a supreme being was already perceived, and this concept of God was expressed through sayings, songs and myths as is still common today. Spirits mediated between God and the people. Ancestors were not considered dead as long as members of the family still remembered them. They took part in the family life and were given food and beverages which they acknowledged in giving consolation and advice in times of need. Offerings were made in thanks to honour them.

The Concept of Time

In Kenya, time is not money. One will quickly realise that the Kenyan concept of time has hardly anything to do with the concept of time in the modern world. It is based on tradition. Time was not a mathematical unit, but a succession of events in the past, the present and in the predictable future. Time was to be lived and experienced, until it became a meaningful and real fact of life.

The way time was measured depended on the people's economic system. Farmers associated certain months with certain events. Thus, the month of May was called ''grain of the ear,'' because the grain is ripened. June might be called ''smeary mouths'' since during this time the children ate the fresh grain and ran about with smeary mouths. Visitors should accept this different concept of time; otherwise, they will be constantly irritated since Kenyans always seem to be unpunctual.

The Concept of Evil

Strokes of fate such as problems at work, illness, infertility and death were treated quite pragmatically. They were not considered an act of God and by no means arbitrary, but caused by evil powers. Perhaps the ''evil'' neighbour has a hand in it, or one had offended the ancestors ... everything had its cause; and thus, the Kenyan people did not resign to fate but looked for ways to remedy the situation as quickly as possible — by appeasing God, the spirits or the ancestors with offerings or purification rites.

The Healer

Healers still carry the well-known but derogatory label ''medicine men'' — cases of damage or injury were remedied by the traditional healers and learned doctors using herbal medicines. They diagnose the cause of misfortune, apply the appropriate therapy and prevent the evil's return. Some of the procedures, as for example curing a wound by incantation, did not have a medical effect in itself; healers were not only responsible for their patients' physical well-being but their soul's as well. The traditional African concept of evil implied not merely the diagnosis of an attack of malaria for example, but the explanation why this particular patient was bitten by a mosquito. Mystic rites revealed that the mosquito was magically influenced by someone. The healer would offer amulets and medicine as a cure. These concepts are still common in Kenya today.

The Dowry

The common prejudice that young girls in Africa were sold off like cattle to their husbands has come threateningly close to reality in recent times. For this reason, Kenyan newspapers often cover this topic, claiming that parents often take advantage of a situation and force their daughters to leave school and marry an an old, but wealthy man — a development resulting from the economic misery of many Kenyans. Yet, the traditional institution of dowry has nothing to do with a purchase. Not the material but the social aspect was important: the dowry implied not only the transfer of material goods but also the linking of two families and the material security of the newlywed couple. In case the marriage failed and the wife was not at fault, she could start a new life with the dowry given to her family after having been divorced — a type of insurance so to say. However, when the parents demand money instead of cattle, the original significance of the dowry is lost.

The women's necklaces are by no means always valuable: cheap, colorful glass beads are becoming increasingly popular

Polygamy

If financially feasable, a man would marry more than one woman. This was the custom with all subcultures in pre-colonial Kenya. Through his wives' efforts, he would become a wealthy and respected member of the society; they would give him many children and social prestige. Love and romance, however, did not first arrive in Kenya with the first Europeans. In general, it was considered very important that love and respect dominated the relationship between the husband and his first wife, since she was considered his advisor and an equal partner. There was freedom regarding the choice of a partner. Today, it is estimated that 25% of all Kenyans are polygamous. The effect of the modern developments in Kenya is that many girls reject polygamy and prefer living together with the partner of their choice.

Currency

It is absolutely prohibited to bring Kenya shillings (KSH) into or out of the country. One must declare all hard currencies in writing upon entering the country (Foreign

A workday in blue jeans, a weekend in the customary costume: the Samburu perform a traditional dance

Currency Declaration). When exchanging money, this document must be presented, the amount exchanged will then be entered on the form and stamped. When leaving Kenya *(→Entering Kenya),* this form must be presented along with the other travel documents.
→Travel Documents

Customs Regulations

All items for personal use can be legally imported without paying duty. It is prohibited to bring firearms, pornographic materials and drugs into the country. There is a strict prohibition on the export of all kinds of hunting trophies or other animal products like fur coats, ivory and snail shells or other seashells.

Diani Beach *→Beaches*
Driving Licence *→Travel Documents*

Economy

Kenya is a thoroughly agraricultural country. The main agricultural products for the domestic market are corn, wheat, oats and sweet potatoes. Combined with animal products, they form the basis for the nation's food supply. However, it is necessary to import food staples from time to time. The most important commodities produced for the international market are tea, coffee, sisal and pyrethrum (the extract of this flower is a component in insecticides). Since only recently, citrus fruits, flowers and different kinds of vegetables are also produced for the export market.
The Kenyan government continues to vehemently pursue the industrialisation of the country. Up until now, the motto has been "substitution of imports" which means that all goods which have had to be imported until present are to be produced domestically. Today, plastic products, fertilisers, furniture, clothing, cigarettes, food and canned goods are produced in Kenya. In addition, breweries, sugar plants, steel mills and assembly plants for cars and radios as well as sawmills supplement the Kenyan economy. An export-oriented industry does not yet exist, apart from being able to handle the first phases of processing tea and coffee. The economic growth slowed from 5.2% to 4.5% in 1989, and in 1990/91 the government was forced to acknowledge a stagnation level hovering around 3.5%. Kenya still has to combat its enormous budget deficit and is more dependent on foreign moneies than ever before. The concept of a mixed economy developed by the government did not improve the situation. There are only 100,000 new jobs for

half a million graduates. An increase in wages is immediately eaten up by the inflation.

Tourism and related services has become an indispensable source of national income. After 1985 (with more than 500,000 visitors, the best year ever for Kenya's tourist industry), travel agencies now speak of a sort of saturation point as far as lions and elephants are concerned: the tourists seem to have had enough of East Africa, not lastly because of the AIDS epidemic and disturbing reports of assaults on travellers. In the meantime, the number of visitors has once again increased, though the numbers of 1985 could not be attained.

Eldoret

(population: 35,000; elevation: 2,100 metres/6,890 feet)

Eldoret (originally Eldare, Eldaret) is a friendly small town surrounded by the lush Uasin Gishu plateau. The fertile soil surrounding the town is the tribal territory of the Kalenjin speaking Nandi *(→People),* whose warriors put up bitter resistance to the British colonial administration up to the 1920's. The first Europeans ever to arrive at this area were the Africaans, fleeing from the Boer Wars in South Africa at the beginning of this century. They came to the region with their ox-drawn carts via Rhodesia (now Zimbabwe). In 1912, the British turned Eldoret into an administrative outpost. The land was distributed among further white settlers, and the town became a hub of the so-called White Highlands.

There are hardly any touristic sights. The town serves as a transit station for travellers on their way up to Uganda or to *→Lake Turkana.* The town's profile is determined by processing industries (among others, leather products) and the Rivatex textile mill, the largest employer in this area. Eldoret is an aspiring town, as is impressivly demonstrated by the newly founded Moi University.

Eldoret / **Practical Information**

Accommodation

Sirikwa Hotel, P.O. Box 3361, Tel: 31655, £13/£16.50 ($25/$31).

Highlands Inn, P.O. Box 2189, Tel: 22092, £13/£16.50 ($25/$31).

New Wagon Wheel, P.O. Box 503, Tel: 22753, £8/£10 ($12.50/$18.50)

New Lincoln, P.O. Box 551, Tel: 22093, £8.35/£11.50 ($15.50/$22)

The last two hotels are idyllic, although somewhat dilapidated houses, dating back to the colonial period. It is possible to camp in the garden at the New Wagon Wheel. More simple hotels are located near the marketplace.

Restaurants: Sirikwa Hotel serves excellent cuisine.

There are several good restaurants in the Eldo Centro supermarket on Uganda Road.

Banks: Barclay's Bank, Uganda Road corner of Kenyatta Street, open Monday to Friday from 8:30 am to 1 pm, Saturday 8:30 to 11 am.

Postal Service: Uganda Road, open Monday to Friday from 8 am to 5 pm, Saturday from 9 am to noon.

Car Rental: Mc Naughton's, P.O. Box 717, Tel: 22464, Kisumu Road The AA (→*Automobile Clubs)* is located in the Oloo Street.

Shopping: Eldo Centro supermarket, Uganda Road.

Juma Hajee's, Oginga Odinga Street.

Transportation: Buses depart daily to Kitale, Kisumu and Nairobi from the bus station at the marketplace. Three times a week (Wednesday, Saturday, Sunday) to Nairobi by train. Air Kenya Aviation flies twice a week to Nairobi.

Electricity

The electrical current is 223 to 240 volts; electrical sockets are tripolar. Be aware that even in the large tourist hotels an adaptor may be necessary. Given the circumstances, it may also be useful in the lodges in the national parks. Most of the lodges are equipped with their own electrical generators, but these do break down sometimes.

Eliye Springs →*Lake Turkana*

Embassies

Australia:
Development House
Moi Avenue, P.O. Box 30360
Nairobi, Kenya
Tel: 374666

Canada:
Comcraft House
Haile Selassie Avenue, P.O. Box 30481
Nairobi, Kenya
Tel: 334033

United Kingdom:
Bruce House
Standard Street, P.O. Box 30465
Nairobi, Kenya
Tel: 335944

United States:
Corner of Moi Avenue and Haile Selassie Avenue
P.O. Box 30137
Nairobi, Kenya
Tel: 334141

Emergencies

An emergency might grow into a mid-sized catastrophe in Kenya, and often the →*police* even make things worse. It is better to practice precaution and to be as careful as possible to avoid a potential emergency. If there is an accident, dial the emergency number 999 — the same all over the country — be prepared for the fact that the police will not come immediately.

Entering Kenya

Already upon entering Kenya *(→Travel Documents)*, one should note that an airport tax of US$20 (or the equivalent in any another "hard" currency) is levied for one's departure. The amount changes constantly, but it never decreases. Thus, one should check into this in advance.

Entertainment

Kenya is not a cultural centre like New York, London or Paris. A cliché? Possibly, but some visitors will only become aware of this fact when they decide to visit a theatre performance or a concert in the evening. This type of entertainment is limited to the capital city of Nairobi. This political and economic centre of the country is also its cultural heart. Yet, the quality of the presentations does not meet international standards. The newspapers will inform the reader when and where these events take place.
Since there are innumerous good to very good restaurants in Nairobi, Mombasa and along the coast, it is not surprising that the night life revolves around eating and drinking. In fact, one can eat out every evening at a different place and set off on a culinary round-the-world tour. Visitors who would like to get to know more

of the Kenyan night life can take a taxi to one of the numerous discotheques or night clubs. Those who enjoy African pop music can visit one of the numerous "day & night clubs," located in every larger city. Live concerts with local artists also take place here often.

Gedi

The most famous city of ruins along the East African coast is located 103 kilometres (64 miles) north of Mombasa close to Malindi. Next to Fort Jesus, it is the most popular destination for excursions.

This city was founded at the end of the 13th century and reached its peak during the 15th century. In the 17th century, the town was deserted by its inhabitants — the reasons remain a mystery. All that is known today in regard to the inhabitants of Gedi is that they were of the Islamic faith and (most probably) belonged to the Swahili population of the coast. It also renmains a secret why this town was founded so far from the sea at a point lacking strategical significance. The theory that these were people from Malindi who settled here because they fell into conflict with their sheik, hay yet to be proven. Gedi seems to have been less important since it is neither mentioned in Portuguese nor in Arabic historical documents. Nevertheless, the inhabitants of Gedi were a prosperous and cosmopolitan people, as evidenced by the impressive ruins of the mosque and the palace as well as by the shards of porcelain and a pair of Venetian scissors from the 16th century. Today, gigantic baobabs grow between the foundation walls. Their foliage covers the entire grounds, lending a mysterious atmosphere to the park. At the entrance, a small museum informs visitors on the background of the excavations up to the latest developments in research.

Geography

Kenya measures 582,646 square kilometres (224,960 square miles) in area, the same size as Spain and Portugal combined. The coast is 400 kilometres (250 miles) long. In the western portion of the country is the massive Lake Victoria — the largest freshwater lakes in Africa. Kenya's neighbours are Uganda, Tanzania, Ethiopia and Somalia.

In addition to the world famous national parks, the true attraction of this country is the unparalleled variety of landscapes. Kenya is a continent in microcosm. From sunbathing on the fantastic beaches to hiking through the perennial ice of Mount Kenya and exploring the hostile deserts north of Isiolo — everything is possible here. The highlands near Nairobi and west of Mount Kenya confront visitors with astounding landscapes — lush meadows and dense pine forests — making visitors forget that the equator runs directly through this country.

The East African Great Rift Valley is of special geological interest. This is part of a zone in the earth's crust with seismic disturbances. This area stretches from Mozambique to the Near East, with a total length of 4,000 kilometres (2,500 miles). The rift's impressive formations can be seen near Nairobi, where its edges plunge up to 1,000 metres (3,280 feet). Lakes containing a high concentration of soda (like Lake Nakuru, Lake Baringo and Lake Turkana) and volcanoes (Mount Longonot, Mount Suswa and Menengai among others) are evidence of a fissure in the earth's crust on the floor of this rift: geologically speaking, two continents are drifting apart. The impressive Aberdare mountain range (Nyandarua Range) *(→Aberdare National Park)* and the Ngong Hills near Nairobi are considered the volcanic boarders.

A savanna belt runs through the central regions of Kenya. This is covered with acacia trees, thorny shrubs and robust bunch grasses. To the north and east, the vegetation becomes increasingly sparse until plant life ceases to exist entirely — with the exception of a few small oases. This region was given the name the Northern Frontier District by the British colonial administration and is almost as large as Italy. This hostile environment can, however, provide only a meagre sustenance for around 800,000 nomads.

Guest Houses *→Accommodation*

Health Insurance

Hospital costs, doctor's fees and expenses for medication incurred during holidays must be paid in cash in Kenya Shillings. Upon returning home, invoices are submitted to one's health insurance company for reimbursement. In order to avoid misunderstandings, the invoices should be written in English. Furthermore, the name, place and date of birth, date, diagnosis, treatment and the doctor's signature must be included.

Ask the health insurance company about specific conditions regarding the reimbursement. It may be wise to take out a supplemental travel health insurance policy at one of the larger travel agencies.

Hell's Gate National Park

Thi is one of the smallest national parks in Kenya, and — apart from the Saiwa Swamp National Park near Kitale — the only game reserve which can be scouted out on foot. A walk among the zebras, Eland and Kuku antelopes, giraffes and hoardes of baboons makes for a memorable experience. It is advisable to keep one's distance from the aggressive African buffalo.

The park was founded in 1984 and encompasses the Njorowa Gorge, slicing several hundred miles through the earth — somewhat remeniscent of the Grand Canyon. The floor of this gorge is framed by bare rock rising vertically out of the ground. Shortly beyond the entrance to the park, the visitor will pass Fischer's Tower, a stony lava needle standing in solitude. This is the remnant of a small prehistoric volcano. It was named after the German natural historian, G. A. Fischer, the first European to explore this "gateway to hell" in 1883. A small colony of badgers has settled down here, making this their home. After walking 12 kilometres (7½ miles) along the gradual slope, the trail narrows, decending steeply to the floor of the gorge. At the end of the path are hot springs and a small thermal power station.

No trousers but a bicycle — the Masai choose which progressive developments they accept

The road to Hell's Gate National Park begins in Naivasha *(→Naivasha)* at Lake Naivasha, heading along the South Lake Road up to a small electricity station. There, one turns left and follows the road up to the park entrance. It is advisable to take a taxi from Naivasha to the park.

History

East Africa is the ''cradle of the human race.'' Ten to twenty million years ago the ''Proconsul,'' a common ancestor of humans and the great apes, populated the vast savanna regions of Kenya. After having found the remains of the so-called ''homo erectus'' (a humanoid capable of walking erect) the question of the ''missing link'' remained unanswered. The anthropological duo, Mary and Louis Leakey (whose family is one of the most respected in Kenya) discovered a human skull in the Olduvai Canyon in northern Tanzania at the beginning of the 1960's. This skull dates back 75 million years. Obviously, this humanoid already used tools; thus, he was called Homo habilis, referring to technical capability. In the same sedimentary layer, the Leakeys found the remains of a 10 million-year-old Australopithecus, which confirmed the theory that prototypes of the various stages in human development did not live consecutively but existed concurrently. Richard Leakey, the son of these two anthropologists and now the director of the National Museum in Nairobi, could support this thesis with sensational finds at Lake Turkana, the first during the 1970's. Other Kenyan excavation sites at which prehistoric bones and tools are still being uncovered are *→Olorgesaille* and *→Kariandusi.*

This implies that Kenya has been populated since the very beginning of human existence. Eight thousand years ago, humans learned to catch fish, 3,000 years ago they had knowledge of agriculture and animal husbandry. Long before the birth of Christ, the Iron Age succeeded the New Stone Age, and during this time, Bantu-speaking farmers from the West settled into the highlands and coastal regions. At the same time Nilotic-speaking livestock breeders from the north emigrated to the expanses of prairies with their vast herds.

Holidays and Celebrations

January 1: New Year's Day
Easter: Good Friday, Easter Monday
May 1: Labour Day
June 1: Madaraka Day (commemorating Kenya's autonomy)
October 20: Kenyatta Day (commemoratinv Jomo Kenyatta's incarceration)
December 12: Jamhuri (Independence Day)
December 25/26: Christmas Day, Boxing Day

At the end of the Ramadan (month of fasting), the Moslems celebrate "Idd-ul Fitr." The exact date cannot be determined in advance since this depends on the day when the new moon becomes visible for the first time. Maulidi, the festival commemorating the prophets' birthday, is celebrated very colourfully on the island of →*Lamu.*

Other events:
January: International Bill Fish Competition in Malindi.
February/March: Mombasa Fishing Festival and Delamere Cup, organised by the Mnarani Fishing Club in →*Kilifi.*
March: Open Gulf Championship of Kenya.
Easter: Kenya Safari Rallye.
May: Kenya 2000, a two-day motor rallye.
October/November: Malindi Fishing Festival.
December: Bahari Club Fishing Festival in Mombasa.

Holiday Apartments →*Accommodation*
Hospitals →*Nairobi, Mombasa*
Identification →*Travel Documents*

Insurance

Before departing for Kenya, it is advisable to ask one's health insurance company, which medical costs they will reimburse and to what degree. Doctor's and hospital fees must be paid in cash in Kenya. Be sure to ask for a detailed and legible invoice in English, which states the doctor's diagnosis, treatment and the exact amounts paid. This should then be sent to one's health insurance company. If necessary, taking out a supplenmental health insurance policy should be considered. This can be combined with luggage insurance and is available at most travel agencies.

International Press

All international newspapers and magazines are available in the book stores of Nairobi and Mombasa. These are also sold on the streets of the city. Sometimes the larger newspapers are not delayed more than one day.

Kakamega Forest

The Kakamega Forest is located near the administrational centre of the Western Province, Kakamega (population: 40,000). The forest, originally part of a gigantic jungle covering the entire region of Equatorial Africa, is one of the last rain forests in existence in East Africa. The increase in population and lack of land pose a threat to the future of this lush, tropical paradise. In the meantime, it confronts visitors with the typical rain forest vegetation, including giant trees towering 60 metres (200 feet) and the multi-storeyed, opaque ceiling of perennial foliage. Dozens of different kinds of orchids and ivy grow in the shade of the trees while the treetops are populated by numerous clamouring hordes of apes, turacos and parrots. Small pathways lead through the forest.

Accommodation:

Golf Hotel, c/o P.O. Box 42013 Nairobi, Tel: 29751/23488/330820,
£13.50/£16.50 ($25.50/$31).

Kariandusi

Kariandusi is an archeological site where prehistoric finds have been discovered (open daily from 8 am to 6 pm).

During the years from 1928 to 1947, the archaelogist Louis Leakey and his assistants were excavating here. They found obsidian stone tools, which served the homo erectus in skining and cutting his prey one million years ago. A number of stone balls which could be thrown over long distances by means of leather slings were also unearthed. The fact that traces of a permanent settlement could not be found leads to the conclusion that Kariandusi was a type of working place. After having successfully concluded the hunt, the people came to this place to make the necessary tools on site. The most important pieces found during these excavations are exhibited in a small museum.

Kericho

(population: 35,000; altitude: 1800 metres/5,890 feet)

This tidy city in western Kenya is the capital of the Kipsigis people *(→People)*, located in the centre of the largest area of tea plantations in East Africa. A warm climate and daily rainfall allow for the harvest of tea during the entire year. Systematic cultivation of tea for the world market began in 1922, when the British Brooke Bond Group put the first plantations into operation. The dense forests were cleared to make way for the tea bushes. Today, seemingly endless rows of these bottle-green plants pruned waist-high cover the gently rolling hills. These are

harvested every two weeks by hand since only the top leaves are picked. This guarantees the internationally acknowledged premium quality of Kenyan tea. The total tea production is still dominated by a few huge plantations, employing up to 500 tea pickers. With the beginning of the 1970's, small farms saw an increase in subsidies. Recently, the legendary Tea Hotel has organised interesting sight seeing tours through the plantations and processing facilities. Meanwhile, these tours have been discontinued. The employees of the surrounding small farms, however, are happy to show interested visitors around their fields.
Kericho itself does not offer special attractions, but does differ from the other noisy and mostly chaotic cities of its size with an amiable city centre, blossoming shrubs and trees and meticulously trimmed lawns. An above-average number of Asian families, promenading on the covered streets, lend a Middle-East flair to this city.

Kericho / **Practical Information**

Accommodation

Tea Hotel, P.O. Box 75, Tel: 20280/2, £13.50/£31.25 ($25.50/$16.50). Dates back to the colonial period; this is the top hotel in town and has a swimming pool.
Kericho Mwalimu Hotel, P.O. Box 834, Tel: 20601, £5.50/£7.50 ($10.50/$14.50).
Tas Lodge, Moi Highway (near the Tea Hotel), P.O. Box 164, Tel: 21112, £2.50/£4.50 ($5/$8). Camping in the garden is possible.

Banks: Barclay's Bank and Standard Bank, both located at the Moi Highway towards Kisumu.

Postal Service: Moi Highway, open Monday to Friday from 8 am to 5 pm, Saturday from 9 am to noon.

Restaurants: All hotels mentioned above include a good restaurant with international and native cuisine. In the centre of the city, the solid cuisine of the Mother Hotel is worth a visit.

Shopping: A large variety of vegetables, spices and fruit can be purchased at the marketplace outside the city; Sundays are especially good for a visit.

Transportation: Cross-country buses and matatus operate daily between Kericho and Nairobi, Kisii and Kisumu as well as to all other smaller towns nearby. The bus station and the ticket offices are located on the outskirts of the city, within sight of the marketplace.

Kisii

(population: 38,000; altitude: 1,800 metres/5,890 feet)

Kisii is the capital of the Kisii Province in the extreme southwest of Kenya. This city is also the centre for the Bantu speaking Gusii population. At the beginning

of the 20th century, the Gusii resisted the British colonial army in several wars. The large number of casualties compelled them to submit to the superiority of British armed forces.
Kisii is an interesting town for two reasons: on the one hand, it is located amidst the most densely populated region of Kenya, where more than 600 people per square kilometre live. This is dramatically reflected by the deforested, and intense cultivation (almost to the point of exhaustion) in areas located within a wide radius of the city, as well as by the noisy and hectic city itself. Tea, vegetables and fruit are important sources of income. The second reason is that Kisii is the home of soapstone production, which is mined in the nearby quarries. This especially soft and bright stone is not only used in producing the souvenirs so popular among tourists, but also for making objects with a high artistic value.

Kisii / **Practical Information**

Accommodation

Kisii Hotel, Kisumu Road, £5/£7.50 ($9/$14). Attended parking area.
Kisii Mwalimu Hotel, P.O. Box 1385, Tel: 20691.

Banks: Barclay's Bank, on the Main Street, open Monday to Friday from 8:30 am to 1 pm, Saturday from 8:30 to 11 am.

Postal Service: Post office on the Main Street, open Monday to Friday from 8 am to 1 pm, in the afternoon from 2 to 7 pm, Saturday from 9 am to noon.

Restaurants: Both hotels include acceptable dining rooms. In the centre of the city there are numerous pubs with local flair.

Transportation: Cross-country buses depart to Nairobi several times daily. There are also good connections to →*Kisumu* and →*Kericho.*

Kisite Island

This small island is located in the middle of the Kisite-Mpunguti Marine National Park on the southern coast of Kenya. Avid scuba divers consider this park the most beautiful diving area in East Africa with its crystal-clear water and still untouched coral banks. Simple lodgings as well as camping areas are available on the neighbouring island of Wasini (via →*Shimoni),* where the Mpunguti Restaurant regularly organises full-day diving trips to Kisite Island.

Kisumu

(population: 170,00; altitude 1,130 kilometres/3,707 feet)

Being the third largest city of Kenya and covering an extensive area, Kisumu reminds one more of Central Africa with its shady parks and casually strolling residents than of a noisy city in the Kenyan highlands. Most of the people living in Kisumu belong to the Luo population — numbering 2.2 million, this is the second largest group in Kenya. In the 16th century, they left their homes in the southern Sudan and migrated to the banks of Lake Victoria, where they quickly changed from a nomadic cattle-breeding lifestyle to fishing and farming. Since the missionaries started their work quite early in the western regions of Kenya and in Uganda, a young elite quickly developed among the Luos. Thise clique founded a number of political organisations (among others the Young Kavirondo Association) since the 1920's. With Kenya's independence, a severe conflict arose btween the Luos and the dominating Kikuyu, regarding appointments to key economic and political offices. These conflicts climaxed with the assassination of the popular Luo politician Tom Mboya in 1969. Under president Moi, the Luo were given more political power. Recent developments point to a new type of alliance between the Luo and Kikuyu against the president, who is accused by both peoples of ruling undemocratically as well as of giving preference to the politicians within his own ethnic group, the Kalenjin.

Like most of the Kenyan cities, Kisumu also owes its existence to the Uganda railway. In 1901, the first trains arrived at the banks of Lake Victoria; its destination, a meagre cluster of tents and shacks called Port Florence. From here, people departed for Uganda by steamship. The first settlers had to endure the tropical humidity. Malaria, sleeping-sickness, and bilharziasis raged and claimed many lives. Kisumu experienced an upswing in the 1930's and 40's, when it advanced to the most important inland port in the region. This was to end in 1977, when the East African Community (from which Kisumu had especially profitted as a commercial hub) broke apart. When walking through the dock area with its empty warehouses and the deserted quay walls, one easily can see that the city has not fully recovered from this set-back to this day — this, despite numerous national and international aid programmes. Nevertheless, the residents face their future optimistically since improved relations to the neighbours Uganda and Tanzania also signal new, promising perspectives for their city in the long term.

The true appeal of Kisumu is its peaceful and friendly atmosphere. Everything is much more relaxed, even at the bus station — visitors who do not know their way around can take their time to find the right bus line without being rushed by a honking bus. The largest employers are a cannery, a fishing net factory, a brewery, grain mills and a large bakery. In an industrial park located beyond the Otieno-Oyoo Street, new machine parts are recycled manually from waste products.

Kisumu / **Sights**

Kisumu Museum, Nairobi Road (behind the market), P.O. Box 1779, Tel: 40804. Interesting and appealing exhibits of ethnographic collections with information on the lifestyle of the Kalejin peoples during the pre-European period. The collection of musical instruments includes an artistic Luo harp, a ''nyatiti'' whose sound is similar to that of the West African ''kora,'' which is even used by African pop musicians today.

Kisumu / **Practical Information**

Accommodation

Sunset Hotel, Aput Lane, P.O. Box 215, Tel: 41100, £13.50/£16.50 ($25.50/$31). Modern luxury hotel at the outskirts of the city with a view of the lake. Swimming pool.

Hotel Royale (formerly: New Kisumu Hotel), Kenyatta Avenue, P.O. Box 1690, Tel: 40559. Nostalgic lodging in the British colonial style.

Lake View Hotel, Alego Street, P.O. Box 1216, Tel: 42055.

Various inexpensive lodgings along the Oginga Odinga Road.

Banks Barclay's Bank, Oginga Odinga Road, open Monday to Friday from 8:30 am to 2 pm, Saturday from 8:30 to 11 am.

Entertainment: Flamingo Casino, Jomo Kenyatta Highway, P.O. Box 525, Tel: 40527.

Octopus bottoms up day and night club, Ogada Street, P.O. Box 1329, Tel: 40835. Good atmosphere, cozy roof garden.

Libraries: Kisumu Library, near the bus station, open Monday to Thursday from 9:30 am to 6:30 pm, Friday from 9:30 am to 4:30 pm, Saturday 9 am to 1 pm. British Council, Oginga Odinga Road, P.O. Box 454, Tel: 45004, open Monday to Friday from 10 am to 1 pm and from 2 pm to 5 pm, Saturday from 8:15 am to 12:30 pm.

Postal Service: Post office at Oginga Odinga Road, open Monday to Friday from 8 am to 5 pm, Saturday from 9 am to noon.

Restaurants: Sunset Restaurant (in the Sunset Hotel, see above). Sundays Asian cuisine and barbecue.

Hotel Royale (see above). Saturdays All-you-can-eat buffet.

Alfirose, Oginga Odinga Road, Tel: 41677. Indian-African specialties. Recommendable: Fish filet Masala. Open daily from 10 am to 11 pm, Sundays from 1 to 11 pm.

Mona Lisa, Oginga Odinga Road. Simple cafe and restaurant, Indian vegetarian specialties. Open daily from 8 am to 9 pm.

Shopping: Vegetables and fruit are best purchased at the marketplace near the Jomo Kenyatta Highway. This is the largest of its kind in West Kenya. The Wananchi Craft Shop & Weaving Project, also located at the Jomo Kenyatta Highway, is run by the Catholic Church. Articles from the traditional Luo culture, such as pottery, three-legged chairs and thumb pianos are offered.
Transportation: Kisumu is connected with the other cities of Kenya by a well operating tranportation network. Cross-country buses, the railways and Kenya Airways offer connections to Nairobi and Mombasa several times daily. Departing from the bus station at the Kenyatta Highway, buses also operate to other cities in western Kenya several times daily. The towns on the banks of Lake Victoria (Kendu Bay and Homa Bay among others) are served by antiquated ferries. Tickets are available at the port of Kisumu. Ferries also serve the route to Mwanza and Musoma in Tanzania.

Kitale

(population: 35,000; altitude: 1,890 metres/6,200 feet)
In former times, this city served as a meeting point for white settlers who first came to this area in 1908. Today, Kitale is the capital of the Trans Nzoia District and a centre for fruit cultivation (apples). The city was founded in 1920; in 1925, the city was incorporated into the railway network. The fertile land in the surrounding regions was cultivated and Kitale gained a reputation for its vegetable gardens. Even today, thousands of interested visitors are attracted from all over the country by the extensive agricultural exhibition, taking place every year in October. For travellers, this city with its meticulously painted houses is only of interest as a gateway to the rugged northern regions of Kenya. Only a few miles beyond the city limits, the gardens and pastures give way to the arid savannas, whose hot winds often blow into the city. Kitale is the only city with regular bus service to Ferguson's Gulf at Lake Turkana (via Lodwar). The long trip there has lost much of its adventure since the road had been paved, but still is a challenge to the passengers' physical condition and nerves.

Kitale / **Sights**

Kitale Museum, P.O. Box 1219, Tel: 20670, open from 9:30 am to 6 pm. The museum includes a collection of butterflies, ethnographic exhibitions, a (mostly empty) snake pit and an interesting educational hiking trail. One should not miss the piano and the pieces of old furniture dating back to the settlers' time.

Kitale / **Practical Information**

Accomodation

Hotel Mamboleo Kitale, £3.35/£6.25 ($5/$9.40). Simple and clean.

Excursions: To →*Saiwa Swamp National Park.*

Restaurants: Black Horse Bar & Restaurant. Inexpensive meals and generous portions.

Transportation: Several times daily, buses depart for Lodwar and Ferguson's Gulf at Lake Turkana. Early in the morning, cross-country buses also leave for Nairobi.

Lake Baringo National Reserve

The first European to ever arrive at Lake Baringo was to fall into raptures. In 1892, the Englishman J. W. Gregory noted that the lake is one of the most beautiful places of Africa. Covering an area of 130 square kilometres (50 square miles) and located on the floor of the East African Rift, this lake could preserve its charm up to present. It is surrounded by dry thorn bush vegetation, and depending on the position of the sun, shimmers in crimson to rust colours at its surface when coming from →*Naku-ru.* The dark eastern rim of the rift makes an impressive backdrop for this beautiful oasis. The main attractions are the 448 documented species of birds, some of which are indiginous only to this lake. Its abundant fish population attracts not only ospreys, pelicans and cormorants, but also herons, African eagles and various kinds of kingfishers. With some luck, the very rare hammerhead can be spotted. This bird builds nests measuring up to 2 metres (6.5 feet) in diameter. Many hippopotamuses live in the broad reed belt, which come ashore to graze by night. There is also a discernable colony of Baringo crocodiles; these, however, are too small to do any severe harm to humans. In the lake are the Gibraltar Island, a volcanic island with hot springs and a colony of herons, as well as Ol Kokwa with the luxury Island Camp. Both islands are easily reached by motorboat and definitely worth visiting.

The Njemps have settled the land surrounding the lake and are a small group of people related to the Masai, although they are not nomadic. Every morning, the men go fishing on the lake with crude rafts made from branches. One of their villages is open to visiting tourists.

Those visiting the lake can not only enjoy observing birds in their mostly unspoiled natural environment, but also waterskiing and windsurfing, organised by the Lake Baringo Club. Only a few hundred yards from the Club is the famous snake farm of Jonathan Leakey, the son of the famous archeologist couple Louis and Mary Leakey. Here, visitors can observe poisonous snakes being "milked" for venom.

Lake Baringo National Reserve / **Practical Information**

Accommodation

Lake Baringo Club, c/o P.O. Box 47557 Nairobi, Tel: 335807, £32.50/£41 ($61/$77.50). Idyllic hotel located directly at the lakeshore. Swimming pool, boat rental, water sports facilities.

Island Camp, P.O. Box 1141 Nakuru, £36.50/£45 ($68.50/$84). Luxury camping site on the island Ol Kokwe.

There is an inexpensive camping area with sanitary facilities directly next to the Lake Baringo Club.

Transportation: The road from Nakuru to Campi ya Samaki (Fish Camp), a town located at the Lake Baringo, was recently paved. Cross-country buses operate on this route twice a day.

Lake Bogoria National Reserve

Visitors on their way to →*Lake Baringo* usually enjoy taking a detour to Lake Bogoria (formerly Lake Hannington). Covering an area of only 34 square kilometres (13 square miles), it is one of the smallest lakes in the East African Rift. This is an insider tip which never seems to disappoint visitors since it is visited only seldom. The lake offers a completely different way of experiencing nature than does Lake Baringo, almost within view from this point. Directly on its eastern shore, the rocky walls of the Laikipia Escarpment tower to a height of 600 metres (1,968 feet) above sea level, a rugged and romantic backdrop for the pink flamingos, tens of thousands of which visit this lake regularly. At the southern end of this lake, measuring 17 kilometres (10½ miles) in length, sulphurous hot springs and geysers bubble out of the earth spouting boiling water up to 5 metres (16 feet) into the air. Not far from here is a wonderful place to have a picnic. The springs are a popular destination for excursions undertaken by Asian families from →*Nakuru,* located about 60 kilometres (37½ miles) away. This lake is attributed with healing properties.

It is extremely unpleasant and possibly highly dangerous, if an all too curious tourist gets too close to the boiling springs and slips on its rim. Some tourists tried to boil eggs in the hot water, fell into the springs and suffered critical burns.

The turn-off on the road B4 coming from Nakuru leads to Lake Bogoria. It has recently been paved up to the springs. The lake as well as the surrounding area — a habitat for the rare kudus — has meanwhile been declared a national reserve. There are three self-catering camping areas at the lake, one with sanitary facilities.

Transportation: The lake is only accessible by car.

Lake Naivasha

With the exception of Lake Baringo, Lake Naivasha is the only freshwater lake on the East African Rift. Located only 90 kilometres (56¼ miles) from →*Nairobi,* this picturesque tract of land is a favourite destination for weekend trips with city residents. For this reason, it should be avoided during weekends. Two comfortable hotels at the lakeside as well as two self-catering camping areas are open to all visitors.

The name "naivasha" comes from the Masai word "e-naiposha," which means as much as "that which rises and falls." The level of the water does in fact constantly rise and fall: old boundary posts dating back to the settlers' time, protrude from the water more than 100 metres (327 feet) from the shore. These are evidence that the lake was much smaller in the 1950's than it is today. At present, the water level is once again on the rise. Pelikans and cormorants have settled on the east side of the lake, especially near the hotel. A total of 340 different kinds of birds have been spotted; among them, various species of kingfishers, carrion eating marabus, delicate love-birds and sea eagles nesting high in the upper branches of the fever acacias. A small herd of rhinoceroses lives close to the Fisherman's Camp at the southern shore. Reed bucks, dikdiks, gazelles and pythons can be observed during a walk on Crescent Island, measuring 2 square kilometres (0.8 square miles) in area and located opposite the Lake Naivasha Hotel. This lake is situated at an altitude of 1,850 metres (6,069 feet) above sea level, making it the highest lake in the East African Riff. There is sometimes even heavy frost during the early morning hours. Therefore, no crocodiles or any other unpleasant contempories which could take away from enjoying water sports live in this region. The lodgings around the lake rent out rowboats and motor boats, making it possible to explore the lake on one's own. The lake has a surface area of 180 square kilometres (69 square miles) and an average depth of 8 metres (26 feet). Warnings should not be taken lightly: during the afternoon, winds can whip the normally glassy surface of the lake, churning up gigantic breakers. Rowing can quite unexpectedly become a highly dangerous activity.

During a trip around the lake, one experiences the modern Kenya of today as well as the nostalgic atmosphere of the colonial past. Driving along a paved (and later unpaved) road, one first passes the extensive flower fields of the Sulmac plantation, which employs about 4,000 people and produces flowers for the world market. Somewhat farther, hidden in carnations and grapevines (a slightly acidic wine is produced in Naivahsa), one comes upon the former colonial villas. These are still owned by Europeans. The excentric Lord Delamere *(→History)* owned a presumptuous villa on this side of the lake as well. Joy Adamson lived on the western shore, known throughout the world as author of the successful novel ''Born Free'' — the history of Elsa, the lioness. Adamson was killed by a domestic servant several years ago. Today her house ''Elsamere'' serves as a nature conservation centre and is open to visitors during the afternoon.

Lake Naivasha / **Practical Information**

Accomodation

Lake Naivasha Hotel, South Lake Road, P.O. Box 15, Tel: 20013, £36.50/£46.50 ($68.50/$87.50) (enormous discounts during the low season). An charming hotel of the 1930's in the style of British cottages, marvellous garden and excellent cuisine.

Boat trips and bird-watching excursions lead by an ornithologist are offered; camping is possible.

Safari Lodge, South Lake Road, P.O. Box 72, Tel: 20241, more luxurious (and more expensive) than the Lake Hotel. Tennis, rowing, horseback riding. Camping is also possible.

YMCA, South Lake Road, huts and self-catering camping facilities, separated from the lake by a small forest.

Fisherman's Camp, South Lake Road, P.O. Box 14982 Nairobi. Huts and tents up £1.70/$3.15, directly on the lakeshore in an acacia grove. Rowboats are also available.

Excursions: →*Hell's Gate National Park*

Lake Nakuru National Park

The bird sanctuary of Lake Nakuru is located 157 kilometres (98 miles) west of Nairobi. It can easily be visited during a day-trip. Up until only recently, the lake had an international reputation because it was occasionally frequented by up to 2 million flamingos: pictures of pink clouds of the lesser flamings around the lake quickly spread throughout the world. The flamingoes feed on algae which flourished in the alkali-rich water of this lake. During the 1980's, intense rainfall and decreased evaporation caused the water level to rise and a fall in the salt concentration. With this, the flamingos migrated, spreading out over the other lakes in the East African Rift region. Today, the most flamingos can be found at →*Lake Bogoria,* while only a small flock still lives in Nakuru.

Even without its flamingo population, the park is a jewel among Kenyan national parks. More than 400 species of birds have settled on its shores. Among these are cormorants, pelicans, herons, spoonbills, ibises, storks, marabus, kingfishers, eagles, buzzards, diving ducks and snake birds. Between September and April, the lake is also a favourite station for migratory birds from Europe. In 1974, the hinterland was annexed into the park, so that it now encompasses of a total area of 200 square kilometres (77 square miles). The lake's eastern shore is bordered by rugged, towering rocks, on which the world's largest primeval candelabra euphoria forest grows. The hinterland to the north and the south of the lake is covered by acacia woods, swamps and small streams — a habitat for the rare Rothschild giraffes, lions and leopards as well as reed bucks and various kinds of antelopes. The Baboon Rocks rise up on the western shore of the lake. This is a steep, rocky slope inhabited by baboon hordes and pythons. Looking down from its highest point, one has a wonderful view of the lake. The biggest attraction of the park, however, are the black rhinoceroses; a reserve was set up in the southern portion of the park exclusively for these animals, which required a large

The vegetation at Lake Turkana is anything but lush

sum of money. In hopes of protecting them from poachers, these endangered animals are guarded around the clock by the rangers.

Lake Nakuru National Park / **Practical Information**

Accommodation

Lion Hill Camp, c/o P.O. Box 30680 Nairobi, Tel: 333233, £41/£49 ($77/$92), offering substantial discounts during the low season. Not a camp, but a cluster of luxury bungalows, nestled against the mountain slope offers a magnificent view of the lake. Restaurant, sauna, swimming pool.

Lake Nakuru Lodge, c/o P.O. Box 70559 Nairobi, Tel: 24998/26778, £35/£47 ($65/$88). Having been expanded several times, this was originally the country estate of the of the eccentric Lord Delamere, a leader of the white settlers during the colonial time *(→History).*

There are several camping sites, one with sanitary facilities at the main entrance.

Lake Turkana

For frequent visitors to Kenya, the country only begins north of Mount Kenya, far from the tourist tracks. Up to the Sudan and Ethiopia, there are only thorn bush savannas, semi-arid and arid deserts, bizarre rocky islands and a few tiny oases, which are bases crucial to the survival of the nomadic Samburu, Rendille, Turkana and Gabbra peoples.

In total, less than one million people live in this hostile wasteland. The British Colonial Administration was not interested in the ''Northern Frontier District''; it was never of any economic importance, and its population was anything but hospitable. The mistrusting Turkana could only pacified in the 1920's. Having to work in the north was similar to a disciplinary transfer for Kenyan teachers and civil servants. After 1963, the neighbouring state Somalia claimed the territory, tipped off by the Somali people who live in the eastern regions of the Northern Frontier District. The bloody Shifta wars to follow were only to be ended without a victor. This is now a thing of the past, but the roads are still not entirely safe; the strong military presence along the most important routes is visible proof. Those who want to explore this region on their own with a rental car (choose a jeep with four-wheel-drive, and bring along tools, sufficient water and gasoline) should by all means join one of the convoys of buses and trucks which gather in all of the larger villages. A trip through the Northern Frontier District still has its own special appeal. Instead of noisy cities, one experiences the silence of the desert; the overpopulated highlands make way for the vast, arid savannas and a seemingly endless sky.

This trip is not meant for people in a hurry to get somewhere. One has to allow ample time. Breakdowns are common and the rare but heavy rains can turn dry riverbeds into impassable currents within only a few hours. Those who do not think they are absolutely capable of undertaking such an adventurous tour, can take part in a camping safari organised by one of the safari agencies in Nairobi. These agencies arrange exciting trips by truck up to the Lake Turkana and even further on a regular basis.
The Lake Turkana — formerly Lake Rudolph — is so remote that it is difficult to set up an infrastructure for tourism. The heat is also unbearable for many tourists, scaring visitors off from this region. Thus, even in the future, the lake will not suffer the fate of other tourist centres in Kenya. Measuring 250 kilometres (156¼) in length and with a width of up to 55 kilometres (34½ miles), Lake Turkana is the world's largest desert lake which is permanently filled with water. A few thousand years ago, it even extended down as far as *→Lake Baringo,* and was also connected to the Nile. This explains the large stock of Nile perch in the lake. Above all, the fascination of this lake is based on the fantastic play of colours of its surface: depending on the position of the sun, the colour shimmers from grey to jade green to a bright blue, framed by lunar landscapes of yellow wasteland, grey-black lava slopes and extinct volcanoes radiating the desert heat. A desolate, but at the same time fascinating area, this lake was first discovered in 1888 by an Austrian expedition, guided by Duke Teleki. It gained renown beyond the borders of Kenya after sensational finds of fossils and bones were unearthed in Koobi Fora, a prehistoric excavation site on the eastern shores. It was here that Richard Leakey, director of the Nairobi National Museum, found the skull of "homo habilis" dated at 2.6 million years which is about 850,000 years older than other similar finds in the Olduvai Gorge in Tanzania *(→History).* Interesting discoveries in recent years have supported the theory that the long-sought cradle of humanity was indeed at Lake Turkana. Of the three islands in the lake, the volcanic Central Island *(→Central Island National Park)* is the most interesting.

Lake Turkana / **Sights**

El Molo Village

Located somewhat north of Loyengalani and nestled in a valley on the shores of the lake is the village of the El Molo. With only 500 members, this is the smallest ethnic group in Kenya. Little is known of their origin and culture. They have given up their own language, a Kushitic idiom and now they speak the language of the Samburu, a culture which they have adopted as well. Gathering and fishing form the basis of their existence. Recently, they also secure supplemental income through safari tourism. Visitors are allowed to visit the village and take pictures if they pay a small gratuity to the village chief. The island opposite El Molo is accessible by motorboat. There a also quite a few Nile crocodiles living here.

Sibiloi National Park

Located four hours north of Loyengalani, this park was founded in 1973, is only accessible with a four-wheel-drive vehicle. This park covers an area of 1,600 square kilometres (624 square miles) and consists of desert. The main attractions here are the prehistoric excavation sites — above all the world-famous Koobi Fora. The interesting pieces found here, can be seen in the National Museum in Nairobi. Supposedly, big game still inhabits the park. Visitors have reported seeing elephants, lions, zebras and giraffes. A large herd of rhinoceroses lives at the sea shore under legal protection. There are no lodgings for an overnight stay in the park.

Lake Turkana / **Practical Information**

Accommodation

Oasis Lodge, c/o P.O. Box 34464 Nairobi, Tel: 751190/750036, £43/£58.50 ($81/$110). This lodge located near Loyengalani, the only larger settlement at the eastern shore, is extremely expensive, since its supplies are flown in from Nairobi. This lodge offers a swimming pool, boat trips to the southern island and fishing trips. There are two camping areas not far away from the lodge, with showers, a simple restaurant and a small bar.

Transportation: Cross-country buses operate from Nairobi, →*Naivasha* and →*Nyahururu* to Maralal. From there, trucks rumble thorugh Baragoi and the South Horr oasis to Loyengalani. The same route is used by the rented car drivers and the camping safari agencies *(→Travel in Kenya).*

Lake Turkana / **Western Shore**

Sights: →*Central Island National Park*

Lake Turkana — Western Shore / **Practical Information**

Accommodation

Lake Turkana Fishing Lodge, P.O. Box 509 Kitale, £19.50/£28 ($36.50/£52.50). Swimming pool, water sports facilities, boat trips to the →*Central Island National Park.*

Transportation: There are buses operating from →*Kitale* to Lodwar on paved roads. From there, buses continue to Kalokol and to the lodge.

Lamu

(population: 10,000)

Studying travel literature on Kenya, the following tip is almost always mentioned: during a tour through Kenya, visit the town and the island of Lamu last! This is good and trustworthy advice. Those who visit Lamu at the beginning of their trip would quite certainly surrender to the laid-back charm of this town with its Islamic flair, forget their travel plans and spend the rest of their holiday in Lamu.

Lamu is the largest town on the archipelago with the same name. This island cluster also includes the islands of Manda and Pate. Supposedly, this group of islands was visited by the seafaring peoples of the Mediterranean and Indian Ocean before the birth of Christ. The earliest archeological finds date back to around 800 A.D., when moorings and Arabian-Persian trade posts gradually gained permanence and grew into villages and harbours. Islamic artisans and the politically persecuted came to the town and mixed with the native Bantu people forming the beginnings of the Swahili coastal culture. In the 16th century Lamu, was said to be the most

The island of Lamu was discovered by seafaring peoples well before the birth of Christ

affluent town along the coast, even outranking Mombasa. Gigantic plantations on the mainland produced grain and fruit, amber; rhinoceros horn and ivory were exported; mangrove wood used in the construction of ships and houses as well as tortoiseshell were shipped off to the Arabian market.

Different from Mombasa, Lamu reached an arrangement with the Portuguese, who ruled the coast during the 16th and 17th centuries *(→History)*. The city flourished during the 17th and 18th centuries. Political power was transferred to a council of elders, the "Yumbe." Commerce, crafts and the arts flourished, and Lamu became the spiritual centre of the Islamic world as well as an important port of transshipment in the Indian Ocean.

Many of the large, coral houses in the district of Mkomani date back to this period. The victorious battle of Shela in the year 1813 marked the prime of the town's influence and at the same time, the end of its political independence. Though they were unexpectedly victorious over the allied troops of Mombasa and Pates, they asked the sultan of Oman for his support afterwards since Mombasa's revenge was feared. The sultan seized the opportunity to strengthen his grip on the coast, an area which he ruled in name only up to this point in time. He moved his court to Sansibar. The massive fort at the marketplace, a sign of Ottoman presence which cannot be overlooked, dates back to the year 1821. Lamu was to see yet another high point in its history: thanks to the efforts of 40,000 slaves, the residents of Lamu became very wealthy. This wealth was transformed into luxurious, multi-storeyed residential buildings, valuable jewellry and wooden carvings. Towards the end of the 19th century, Mombasa and Sansibar gained importance, and commerce increasingly by-passed Lamu. In 1907, slavery was finally abolished in the town, and Lamu fell into slumber for more than 60 years. During this time, only a few Europeans (apart from the British colonial officials) came to this town. It was only towards the end of the 1960's, when mass tourism had long since established itself in Kenya, that the hippies and drop-outs discovered the hidden beauty of Lamu, making it into their own "African Goa" — water mains laid in 1965 and electricity introduced four years later, made their life in paradise much more convenient. After the hippies, the backpack tourists were to arrive and package tourists were flown in for one-day tours. The residents of Lamu have of course adapted to this flood of visitors. Meanwhile, there are numerous hotels, lodges and inexpensive accommodations in town. The tidy sailboats in the harbour depart on fishing trips only at night, in order to transport tourists to the most beautiful places on the archipelago during the daytime.

Lamu has not suffered the fate of total deterioration into a purely tourist culture. Most of the residents working in the tourist sector can still supplement their income with agriculture or fishing. It seems uncertain how long this situation will remain intact. Rumour has it that after the construction of one runway on the neighbour island Manda, a second is planned on Lamu itself. Another rumour persists in regard to plans for a US naval base to be built on Manda...

Lamu / **Sights**

There are no special attractions in Lamu. However, the town is in itself a small treasure chest, whose unique atmosphere preserved from the 19th century can be best discovered on a random walk through the tangled maze of the murky alleyways and narrow passages. Late afternoon is the best time for such a walk since the midday heat is then tempered by a fresh ocean breeze.

Those who lose their way, will still not be lost. One good orientation is to be aware that Lamu is situated on a slope: inland, on a hill sloping down to the ocean. If one heads for the ocean, one will inevitably come to the main street of Lamu, Harambee Avenue (formerly: Usita wa Mui). The residents of the impressive coral buildings are shielded from the eyes of curious strangers and the street noise by thick, windowless walls. The private life of these families takes place mainly within the spacious inner courtyards, which are often accented with flowers and small palms. All rooms look out onto this atrium; in the evening the people sit together on the flat roofs.

Visitors must not fear agressive drivers and stinking buses: there are none in Lamu. The only car on the island District Commissioner's which, however, cannot be used since there are no streets broad enough. Mules, hand carts and one's own God-given legs have been the only means of transportation in this town since time immemorial.

The splendid, multi-storeyed stone buildings with galleries and rounded arches along the harbour promenade are from the period after 1830. Originally, the quay wall led along the Usita wa Mui, but due to the growing mountains of rubbish, it became necessary to reclaim a lot of new territory. The *Lamu Museum* offers interesting insight into the lifestyle during that time (Harbour Promenade, open daily from 8 am to 6 pm, P.O. Box 48, Lamu, Tel: 3037). The Swahili coast culture is the focal point of the exhibition. In addition to a completely furnished Swahili dwelling, clothing and everyday articles, two artfully decorated ''Siwas'' (ceremonial horns) are the showpieces of the museum. Both of these date back to the 17th century and are among the oldest historical musical instruments of Black Africa. The Ottoman *Fort* (mentioned previously) forms the centre of town with its 20 metre (65 feet) high, massive bastion towers. After having been completely restored, it now serves as a museum. Behind it to the right is the *Pwani-Mosque*. Built in 1370, this is the oldest of the 24 mosques of Lamu. Its interior is relatively rustic and can only be entered by men. The largest, and at the same time most beautiful, mosque is the *Rhyadha Mosque* in the Langoni quarter. It dates back to the turn of the century and is the spiritual centre of Lamu. The feast "Maulidi" is celebrated every year at this mosque commemorating the birthday of the prophet Mohammed. Festivities include dancing, music and a ceremonial procession. Behind the Riyadha Mosque is a *Grave Column* from the 14th century. The government declared this a national monument, but nothing was undertaken to change its pitiful condition. There is a market every day on *Government Square* at the base of the fort. Fresh tomatoes, limes, betel nuts, bananas and quite possibly the best mangoes in Kenya are sold here. On Saturdays, auctions take place, visited in large numbers. Up for auction is anything and everything which is thought to have any value, from jeans and toasters to hand-carved beds in the traditional Lamu style.

Magnificent, multi-storeyd stone buildings with galleries make up the profile of Lamu City

Lamu / **Practical Information**

Accomodation

Petley's Inn, P.O. Box 4, Tel: 3048, £13/£16.50 ($25/$31). The most expensive hotel in Lamu and the only place in town where alcoholic beverages are served.

Yumbe Guest House, P.O. Box 81, Tel: 9121-3101, £7.30/£11.50 ($13.50/$22). Beautiful building furnished in the Swahili style, and run by a friendly staff.

New Mahrus Hotel, located next to the Fort, £6/£8.30 ($11/$15.50). The rooms on the top floor are especially recommandable.

Banks: Standard Bank, P.O. Box 100, Tel: 3265, open Monday to Friday from 8:30 am to 1 pm, Saturday from 8:30 to 11 am.

Entertainment: Nightlife counts very little in Lamu. There are two cinemas, which are always well frequented — regardless which movie is shown. An evening in the "Zinj" or in the "Coast-Cinema," an outdoor cinema, will guarantee a completely new atmosphere for taking in a film.

The large mosque on Lamu's neighbouring island of Manda continues to deteriorate

The Social Hall on the northern end of the harbour promenade organizes dances on Saturdays. Once a month, a travelling discotheque makes its stop in Lamu, set up below the new broadcasting station in the southern area of the city.

Postal Service: The post office is open Monday to Friday from 8 am to 12:30 pm and 2 to 5 pm, Saturdays from 9 am to noon.

Restaurants: Ghai's Restaurant, Harbour Promenade. This has been the best address for seafood for years.

Equator Restaurant, Langoni. Serving exquisite cuisine and run by an lovably eccentric Englishman, who welcomes every guest with a handshake.

Coral Rock (formerly Yoghurt Inn), at the northern end of the Usita wa Mui. The fresh crabmeat with melted cheese served under a thatched palm roof, accompanied by descrete rock music makes for an unforgettable experience.

Bush Gardens, Harbour Promenade. Tasty banana pancakes, first-class milkshakes and coconut cake made fresh daily.

Shopping: The wooden carvings of Lamu are highly reputed. At times, the splendid hand-carved doors have been so popular among the Europeans that only half a dozen of them still exist in the town itself. It is worthwhile to browse and rummage through the goods displayed in the shops along the northern end of Usita wa Mui. In addition to beautiful Arabian style furniture, with a little luck one can also still find old coins from the past century used to make jewellery.

The tailors and textile merchants are clustered around the Riyadha Mosque in the Langoni quarter. Here, one can have one's clothing made to measure.

Transportation: Buses depart for Mombasa and Nairobi three times a week. The ticket offices are located on Usita wa Mui. Equator Airlines and Air Kenya fly to Malindi, Mombasa and Nairobi twice a day. The ticket offices are on the harbour promenade.

Excursions: Lamu — this does not only stand for a historical town and excellent cuisine. The island also offers a fantastic and secluded beach measuting 17 kilometres (10½ miles) in length. It will give visitors the feeling of being Robinson Crusoe. Yet, one should not succumb to the euphoria and swim too far out because of the strong undercurrent! Also abstain from bathing nude and show consideration to the Islamic population. Women should not stay at the beach without being accompanied by a man, since there have already been assaults.

A more extensive walk through the betel gardens and coconut palm groves leads to Matondoni at the northern end of the island. The families in this village have been the boat builders of the islands for centuries. With a little luck, the craftsmen might allow the visitors to observe them at work — yet, it is better to ask for permission in advance. This also applies to taking pictures.

One special attraction of Lamu is an excursion with the Arabian sailing boats, the so-called jahazis. Tourists mistakenly call them dhows, a name which refers to a larger type of sailing vessel. However, this term has meanwhile also been adopted by the boat makers themselves. It is no problem chartering a boat. One must merely go to the quay wall, and someone will come to make an offer. The day trips to the neighbouring island of Manda are most popular; this in connection with a visit Takwa, a city of ruins from the 16th century. Concluding the tour is a barbecue on the beach opposite Lamu.

Although no less charming, only few people visit the island of Pate only two hours by boat from Lamu. In former times, the town of Pate was Lamu's main competition, and at times even more affluent and powerful. On the island are ruins and historical monuments important to the Swahili culture. The town of Pate is laid out similarly to Lamu. However, the roads are only made out of packed earth and the facades are not plastered. The effect of this is the continual deterioration of the town since 1813. In contrast to the cautious and reserved attitude of the townspeople of Lamu, the residents of Pate are curious and friendly. They readily lead the visitors to the Nabahani ruins (mosques, grave columns) which was declared a national memorial. Eight kilometres (5 miles) from the town of Pate is Siyu, a religious centre on this archipelago from the 17th to the 19th century. Its residents produced copies of the Koran, bound books and illustrated texts. Even today, they are famous for their leather products. The monumental fort dates back to the Ottoman period and has been completely restored.

There are no hotels on Pate. Those who want to tour on the island, should plan two days into their itinerary. In general, visitors are offered lodging in private homes.

Language

English is spoken everywhere in Kenya. Even more people speak Kiswahili (Swahili for short) which is the everyday language in Kenya. One may safely assume that everyone among the more than 40 ethnic groups in Kenya will speak at least one of these two languages. Most of the Kenyans are — in contrast to many of the foreign visitors — true linguistic masters. Most Kenyans will have a command of three languages: English, Swahili and their native language. Moreover, the idioms of the neighbouring tribes are also understood. Those Kenyans who have regular contact with tourists do not have a problem juggling six to eight languages! In any case, it is certainly not out of place to know a few Swahili words and phrases. This language is understood from the Comoros Islands in the Indian Ocean and well into the interior of central Africa. Swahili developed on the coast over a thousand years ago; a pleasant, harmonious mixture of Arabian and the native Bantu languages with a few words having been adopted from the Portuguese. The name of this language is derived from the Arabian word for coast (''sahil''). The vocabulary consists of many Arabian words; grammar and syntax have remained Bantu.

The pronunciation is — apart from some exceptions, not relevant for speaking the language — relatively easy. Some terms are even already widely known, as for example the beautiful word ''safari,'' meaning travel, ''simba'' meaning lion, ''hatari'' meaning danger and the historically laden word ''bwana'' for master. Even only rudimentary knowledge of the Swahili language make it much easier to establish contact with the local residents and help overcome the cultural distance experienced by both cultural groups. The attempt to express a wish in Swahili often elicits such enthusiasm that it is countered with a spontaneous crash course in this language.

Greetings

In Kenya it is impolite to express wishes without first prefacing these with a greeting.

Milikea and Joseph try their hand at teaching Kiswahili

Common Expressions:

Jambo!	Hello, Hi!
Hujambo, bwana/mama!	Hello, mister/ma'am
Habari? Harari gani	What's new? How are you?
Habari yako/zeno?	How are you (sing.)/you (pl.)

As a sign of respect, older people are addressed with the title ''bwana'' or ''mama'' or ''bibi.'' Peers in the same age group are addressed with ''ndugu'' (brother) or ''rafiki'' (friend).

Older men prefer ''mzee,'' a title of honour.

Habari za safari?	How was the trip?
Habari za njumbani?	How is it going at home?
Habari za kazi?	How is work going?

Questions like these will always be answered with ''good.'' The fact that the reality of the matter is drastically different is only expressed later on in the conversation. Typical answers to these questions include ''nzuri,'' ''salama'' and ''nyema.''

Saying Good-Bye

Kwa heri!	Good-bye
Tutaonana (kesho)!	See you later (tomorrow)!
Nataka (Tunataka) kwenda sasa	I (we) would like to go now
Twendeni!	Let's go!
Safari nyema!	Have a good trip!
Rudini nyumbani salama!	Have a safe trip home!
Lala salama!	Good night!

Useful Phrases

The small word ''kuna!'' (there is/are) is very helpful when one wants to know what there is to eat or whether there is a bus to the next town or village.

Kuna chakula iko hapa?	Do you have anything to eat here?
Kuna wali na nyama?	Do you have rice and meat?
Kuna chai (kahawa)?	Do you have tea (coffee)?
Kuna basi kwenda Nairobi?	Is there a bus to Nairobi?
Ndiyo!	yes!
Hapana!	no!
Hakuna!	No, not at all!

And where? — this can be solved with the little word ''wapi'' (where).

Wapi hoteli?	Where is there a restaurant?
Wapi choo?	Where is the toilet?
Basi kwenda Nairobi wapi?	Where is the bus to Nairobi

Since — at least in the small little villages — life centres around the marketplace, the answer is often:

Sokoni!	At the marketplace!

Numbers

moja	one
mbili	two
tatu	three
nne	four
tano	five
sita	six
saba	seven
nane	eight
tisa	nine
kumi	ten
ishirini	twenty
thelathini	thirty
arobaini	forty
hamsini	fifty
sitini	sixty
sabini	seventy
themanini	eighty
tisini	ninety
mia	one hundred
elfu	one thousand

Small Talk

Tafadhali	Please
Asante sana!	Thank you very much!
Unasema Kiingereza	Do you speak English?
Ninasema Kiswahili kidogo tu.	I speak only a little Kiswahili.
Tafadhali, sema pole pole	Please, speak slowly.
Inaitwa nini kwa Kiswahili?	How do you say that in Kiswahili?
Unajua ...?	Are you familiar with ...?
Hakuna shida/matata?!	No problem!

Ninataka ...	I would like to ...
Sinataka ..	I don't want to ...
Ngojy!	Wait!
Nina (Sina) haraka!	I am (not) in a hurry!
Pole sana!	I'm sorry!
Sawa sawa!	okay!
Safi kabisa!	Great!
Unatoka wapi?	Where are you from?
Mimi ninatoka Uingeresa/Mericani.	I come from England/Mericani.
Je, unaitwa nani?	Say, what is your name?
Jina langu ni ...	My name is ...
Na wewe, je ...?	And yours ...?
Mimi ninaitwa ...	I'm ...

Photography

The reaction of the Kenyans when they notice that a camera lens is pointed in their direction ranges from reluctant to angry. This is not because they fear that the strangers will gain influence over their souls by taking their picture (those days are long since in the past!), but because this is blatant sign of disrespect to a person's dignity. Many are increasingly aware of their poverty and this reaction is quite understandable when confronted by a walkman and a Nikon camera — symbols of wealth and prosperity, if you will. The feeling of helplessness and humiliation lead to hate and aggression. In such cases, understanding and consideration are called for and a willingness to forgo these holiday snapshots.

If one gets to know someone better, then taking their picture is no problem. With complete strangers, one should definitely ask permission and explain why one wants to take their picture.

kupiga picha	to take a picture
Inawezekana kupiga picha ya wewe/zeno?	Would it be possible to take your (sing.)/your (pl.) picture?
Kwa nini?	Why?
Ninataka kuonyesha picha marafiki yangu nyumbani!	I want to show these pictures to my friends at home!

At the Restaurant

Ninataka (mntaka) kula (kunywa) ...	I (we) would like something to eat (drink) ...
Tafadhali lete ...	Please bring ...

chakula ya asubuhi	Breakfast (usually sweet tea and milk)
chakula ya mchana	Lunch
chakula ya jioni	Dinner
chai	Tea
chai ya rangi	black tea (without milk)
kahawa	coffee
Nina (tuna) njaa (kiu)	I (we) are hungry (thirsty)
maji	water
bia	beer
moto	hot
baridi	cold

Note: The Kenyans prefer their beer warm. One must expressly ask for ''cold'' beer (as long as there is a refrigerator).

Tafadhali lete kahawa nyingine.	Please bring another coffee.
Pilau (chai, bia etc.) shillingi ngapi?	How much is the Pilau (tea, beer etc.)?
Lete cheti tafadhali.	Please bring our bill.

At the Hotel

in the larger hotels, it should be no problem communicating in English. In the smaller towns where there are only simple hotels and ''boardings & lodgings,'' a few Swahili phrases can be useful. A sign with the word ''Hotel'' is usually not an accommodation but a snack bar. One should therefore ask straight away for:

mahali pa kulala	accommodation (place to sleep)
Nitaondoka kesho (asubuhi, mchana)	I am leaving tomorrow (morning, afternoon)

Shopping

Ninataka kununua ...	I would like to buy ...
Kanga hii (kikoi hiki) unanza bei gani?	How much is this Kanga (Kikoi)?
Ghali sani!	Too expensive!
Ninataka kanga rahisi (rahisi zaidi)	I would like a cheap (less expensive) Kanga
Sina pesa!	I have no money!
Matunda	fruit
Maembe	mango
Mananasi	pineapple

Machungwa	oranges
Papai	papaya
Mkate	bread
Siagi	butter
Sukari	sugar
Maziwa	milk
shati	shirt, blouse
sketi	skirt
Kikapu	basket
Ngoma	drum

Travelling Around

Buses and Matatus are the most widely used means of transportation in Kenya. The bus stations are usually directly near the marketplaces and because of the bustle and the bus driver's yelling, simply cannot be missed. The destinations are posted in the front windows of the buses.

„I had a farm in Africa ..." Karen Blixen's house near Nairobi has been a museum since 1986

Soko (Stesheni, Hoteli, Posta, Hospitali) iko wapi?	Where is the marketplace (train station, hotel, post office, hospital)?
Ninataka kwenda ...	I would like to go to ...
Basi la kwenda ... litaondoka lini?	When does a bus leave for ...?
Unakwenda wapi?	Where are you going to?
Tikiti bei gani?	How much is the ticket?
Kiti hiki kina mtu?	Is this seat taken?

Travelling by car does mean a great deal of independence and one might find a village where little or no English is spoken...

Kijiji hiki kinaitwaje?	What is this village called?
Je, njia ya kwenda ... wapi?	Say, where's the road to ...?
Kuna petroli iko wapi?	Where can I find petrol?

Minor car problems are a daily occurrence. There are rarely the appropriate spare parts, but the ingenuity of the Kenyan mechanics is limitless. The technical vocabulary comes directly from the English:

Betri	battery
Breki	brake
Petroli	petrol
Gia	gear
Gesi	gas
Redieta	radiator
Klachi	clutch
Gereji	garage
Injiji	engine
Mafuta	oil
Ajali	accident
Tairi	tire
Jeki	jack
Vyombo	workshop
Plagi	(spark)plug

Illness

Ninaumwa	I am ill
Inaumwa sana hapa!	It hurts here!
Nina shida za ...	I have a problem with ...
Kuna daktari hapa?	Is there a doctor here?
Haraka!	Hurry!

Literature

Kenya is *the* travel destination in Africa. Therefore, there are innumerous books on this country — photographic works, travel books and guides, reports on expeditions and exciting novels. In the 1980's Kenyan authors have also gained international reputation.

Since the successful film ''Out of Africa'' with Streep, Redford and Brandauer was shown, the novel with the same title by the Danish author Karen Blixen has gained renown throughout world. Using magnificent images, the novel describes the life in the Kenyan colony. The British author Elspeth Huxley who came to Kenya as a young girl at the beginning of this century, depicted a lovable and slightly ironic picture of the British colonial society in her novel ''Flaming Trees of Thika.'' The third of the three great Kenya authors is Beryl Markham. Her novel ''West with the Night'' which was already published in 1942. It is an exciting biography of a woman, who came to Kenya as a four-year-old girl in 1906, and worked as a farmer, a race horse trainer and as a commercial pilot for postal planes in East Africa. Both, Karen Blixen and Beryl Markham were linked by their deep love for the British adventurer Denys Finch-Hatton. They were part of the refined, slightly decadent circles of the colonial society, which James Fox portrayed. Written with a vengence, yet with a lot of affinity for the people is the novel ''North of South'' (Penguin Books) by the British author Shiva Naipaul.

Two writers especially belong to the classical authors of Kenya: Jomo Kenyatta, who was later elected the first President of Kenya, wrote ''Facing Mount Kenya,'' a passionate monograph on the history and tradition of his people, the Kikuyu. This was published in 1938. Since its appearence, it has repeatedly gone into reprints. Internationally, Ngugi wa Thiongo is Kenya's most widely known author. He is an attentive observer of political developments in his home country, and has authored books critical to the existing political system. He has lived in exile in London for years.

Malindi

(population: 32,000)

Located 120 kilometres (75 miles) north of →*Mombasa,* Malindi is the second largest city on the coast and is also a tourist centre. For a long time, it was notorious as the ''whore house of Africa,'' and had a dubious reputation of being a Mecca for sex tourism. Since the centre of tourism was moved to the Mombasa region, the prostitutes also migrated — and with them, the investors. However, the Giriama stayed. They are the most widely known ethnic group among the Bantu speaking

Mijikenda, consisting of nine tribes (among others Pokomo, Digo, Taita). They can trace their common origin back to a legendary country called Shungwaya. According to ethnologists and linguists, this is assumed to be located in southern Somalia. The Mijikenda arrived at the Kenyan coast more than 500 years ago. Today, they settle along the coast between Malindi in the north and the Tanzanian border in the south. Visitors to Malindi find the Giriama women and their colourful batik cotton clothing especially attractive. The so-called Giriama Dancing Villages, set up especially for tourists, remind one of the great singing and dancing tradition of the Giriama. These villages are not permanently inhabited settlements, but villages with a few round huts trimed to traditions but nevertheless replicas. The supposed authentic lifestyle of Africa is performed daily to busloads of tourists. The historical town Malindi has made the aquataince with both good and bad times. The first reliable source which mentions Malindi is the Arabian traveller Abu al Fida (1273-1331), although Chinese sources report of a town called Mo-Lin located at the East African coast as early as the 9th century, but this is not described fur-

The Kenyan sunset inspired the author Elspeth Huxley to write her book "Flaming Trees of Thika"

ther. What is a historical fact is that there were intensive diplomatic contacts between Malindi and China during the 15th century. In 1417, the fleet of the Eunuch Cheng Ho anchored off the coast near this town to bring back a delegate of the sheik, who had been sent to China to present the Emperor with a live giraffe as a gift three years prior. The town gained affluence through trade with the Far East — and also with India: leopard skins, tortoiseshell, tusks and mangrove wood were highly desired products in China.

In contrast to Mombasa, its traditional competitor, Malindi received the Portuguese very friendly. Vasco da Gama was the first European to ship around the Cape of Good Hope, and was even given a guide for his trip crossing the Indian Ocean to Kalikut (Calcutta). After the sheik (also was the Portuguese governor) had moved with his court to Mombasa at the end of the 16th century, Malindi suffered a rapid decline. When the German missionary Ludwig Krapf visited Malindi in 1845, he had to use a bush knife to fight his way through the town, now overgrown by jungle. In 1861, Malindi was founded a second time by the sultan of Sansibar. Up to the end of the 19th century, an army of slaves worked diligantly on gigantic, new plantations surrounding the town, providing the population of Sansibar with grain, cassava, mangoes, bananas, oranges and coconuts. When slavery was abolished, Malindi suffered a second decline. Only with the arrival of British settlers was this town to flourish once again. Milindi was rediscovered as having great potential as a seaside resort and many settlers chose it as their place of retirement. The oldest hotel here is the Palm Beach Hotel (today Blue Marlin) which was built in 1931. In the 1960's and 70's Malindi became a holiday resort with international renown.

Today's Malindi offers the visitor a hardly digestible mixture of Disneyland and Arabian flair. It is a vivacious town, but the houses and streets are in poor condition. During tourist season *(→Tourist Season)* the tourists take over the town, when mostly white faces can be seen, especially in the north of the town, where boutiques, souvenir shops, restaurants and nightclubs are located.

Malindi / **Sights**

The splendour of the past has hardly left any traces in Melinda. The old town, a confusing maze, mainly consists of flat clay houses. Most of the few stone buildings are not older than 40 years. During the rains, people have to wade knee-deep through muddy water in the alleyways.

South of the harbour basin is the *Vasco-da-Gama-Cross* on a point reaching far into the ocean. It is one of the oldest European remnants in Black Africa. In 1499, the Portuguese seafarers gave it to the sheik of Malindi as a sign of gratitude for his hospitality. It was not very tactful when he at first had the cross (chiselled out of white Lisbon limestone) installed directly in front of the palace of the Mohammedan ruler. This was a little bit too much for the otherwise good-natured sheik. As soon as da Gama had left, the cross was taken down and put up again at its present-day position on the cliffs.

Only a few minutes walk from the cross is the *Portuguese Chapel,* located on the road leading to the fish market. The chapel's exact age is unknown, but a letter from a certain Francis Xavier to Rome determines that it must have been built before 1542. In 1933, a painting of the Holy Virgin was discovered inside below the cross under a thick layer of plaster. The painting was plastered over yet again to protect it from the tropical humidity.

In addition to the simple Jamia Mosque, two *Grave Columns* point back to the Malindi's golden age. The larger dates back to the 15th century; the smaller, to the 19th century. Its Arabian decorum is still quite obvious.

Malindi / **Practical Information**

Accommodation

Eden Roc Hotel, Lamu Road, P.O. Box 350 Malindi, Tel: 0123-20480/1/2, from £11.50/£25 ($22/$46).

The Driftwood Beach Club, P.O. Box 63 Malindi, Tel: 20155, from £11.50/£18 ($22/$33.50). Pleasant atmosphere and inexpensive cuisine directly at the beach.

Scorpio Villas, P.O. Box 368 Malindi, Tel: 0123-20892, 20194. Luxury 4-bed bungalows in the traditional round hut style, from £15.50 ($29).

Ozi's Bed & Breakfast, Seafront Road, P.O. Box 60 Malindi, Tel: 0123-20218, £3.50/£6 ($7/$11)

Glory Guest House, Lamu Road, P.O. Box 994 Malindi, Tel: 0123-20065. Simple, well run hotel, operated by the Glory rental car agency.

Silversands Campsite, P.O. Box 619, Tel: 20412. This camping area is located 2 kilometres (1¼ miles) south of town, directly at the beach.

Banks: Barclay's Bank, opposite Lawford's Hotel, open Monday to Friday from 8:30 am to 1 pm and 2:30 to 7 pm, Saturday from 8:30 to 11 am.

Beaches: South of Malindi is the beach of Malindi. The white sand with a hinterland covered with coconut palms makes for a breathtaking sight. During the tourist season, the beach around the camping area a meeting point for backpack tourists and African travellers; thus, it can get quite crowded at times. Much more peaceful are the well-tended hotel beaches farther north. However, during the rains the mud of the Sabaki River, flowing into the ocean nearby, takes away from swimming.

Car Rental: Glory Car Hire, Lamu Road, P.O. Box 994, Tel: 20065, Ngala Building. Cars, motorcycles, bicycles.

Excursions: →*Gedi.*

Night Life: Night life centres around the hotel discotheques in the northern districts of Malindi. Some places present the so-called Giriama dances, which are, however, only a weak imitation of the singing and dancing tradition of the Giriama people. These sometimes even pass the limits of good taste.

Restaurants: There are some attractive alternatives to the restaurants of the better hotels (see above) in the north of Malindi.

Metro Restaurant, near the fish market. A rustic restaurant in the Metro Hotel. Inexpensive fish dishes in a colonial-time atmosphere.

Baobab Cafe, near the fish market. Serving local cuisine, this is a meeting place for the backpack tourists.

Stardust, Lamu Road. Exquisite cuisine.

Palm Garden, Lamu Road Bar with a peaceful atmosphere and excellent fish dishes prepared with a generous portion of garlic.

Sports and Recreation: Almost all hotels are equipped with tennis and squash courts. The beach resort of Malindi emphasises water sports. Hotels offer the entire range of water sports, from windsurfing to snorkelling and water-skiing and even parachuting. Glass-bottom boats await passengers for a trip to the coral reefs in the nearby *Malindi Marine Park* located south of Malindi. The park entrance is at Casuarina Point along the southbound street. Tickets can be purchased at the entrance as well as from peddlars on the beach.

Transportation: Cross-country buses go to Mombasa and Nairobi several times daily. Buses to Lamu depart shortly after sunrise. The little airport is located almost 3 kilometres (2 miles) to the south. There are flights to Mombasa and Nairobi two times daily. Tickets are available at the Cooper Skybird Office, Lamu Road, P.O. Box 146, Tel: 20860.

Maps

Maps are available in every book store. However, many of the maps are not up to date. Recommandable is the ''Kenya 1:1,100,000 Nelles Map'' with a lot of information and maps of Nairobi and Mombasa on the back.

Detailed maps of regions especially interesting for tourists and the national parks are published by the Kenyan Survey Department, and are available in the book stores in Nairobi *(→Nairobi)*. However, only as long as supplies last. With some luck, a map can also be purchased at the entrances to the national parks.

Marsabit National Park

Even according to Kenyan standards, Marsabit is one of the most remote and least visited national parks. Covering an area of 592 square kilometres (231 square miles) it is located at the crest of Mount Marsabit (1,700 kilometres/5,577 feet in altitude). Mount Marsabit rises like a cool green island the sweltering desert heat 1,000 metres (3,281 feet) below in the Northern Frontier District *(→History)*. In the shade of the seemingly impenetrable jungle, more than 400 counted kinds of birds live amidst the beard moss, including no less than 50 kinds of birds of prey. The special attraction of the park are the elephants. These are considered the largest elephants on the African continent. The most famous elephant of Marsabit was Ahmed, an elephant bull, who had a sort of symbolic value and was under the personal protection of Jomo Kenyatta. Ahmed's successor is Mohammed. Each of his gigantic tusks is said to weigh 45 pounds. He takes a great deal of advantage of the preferential treatment given him when he visits the domestic gardens in Marsabit City from time to time — never running the risk of being shot. Typical for northern Kenya are the widespread giraffe and the Grevy zebra. Even during the dry season, one can only travel through the park with an off-road vehicle since there are sometimes extremely steep grades. Those who do not travel to Marsabit with their own car, can rent a car with a driver at the park lodge. In contrast to other parks in Kenya, one can leave the car here.

A good vantage point to observe animals is at the numerous "gofs" which are extinct craters along the road to Marsabit City. The Gof Redo, located outside of the park on the road to Moyale is 1.5 kilometres (almost 1 mile) in diameter and 200 metres (654 feet) deep. It is famous for the eagles and rare lammergeiers, whose eyries are attached to the edge of the crater or directly below it. The upcurrents in the crater are so strong that a hat thrown into the crater sails back to its owner like a boomerang — a popular trick performed by the native guides.

Marsabit National Park / **Practical Information**

Accommodation

Marsabit Lodge, c/o P.O. Box 42013 Nairobi, Tel: 29751/330820, £16.50/£27.50 ($31/$52). A hardly frequented lodge with modern standard located 3 kilometres (almost 2 miles) from the park entrance at a small lake.

It is possible to camp on the area of the lodge as well as at the idyllic Lake Paradise, a crater lake. Those who want to stay overnight here will be assigned a ranger for personal protection.

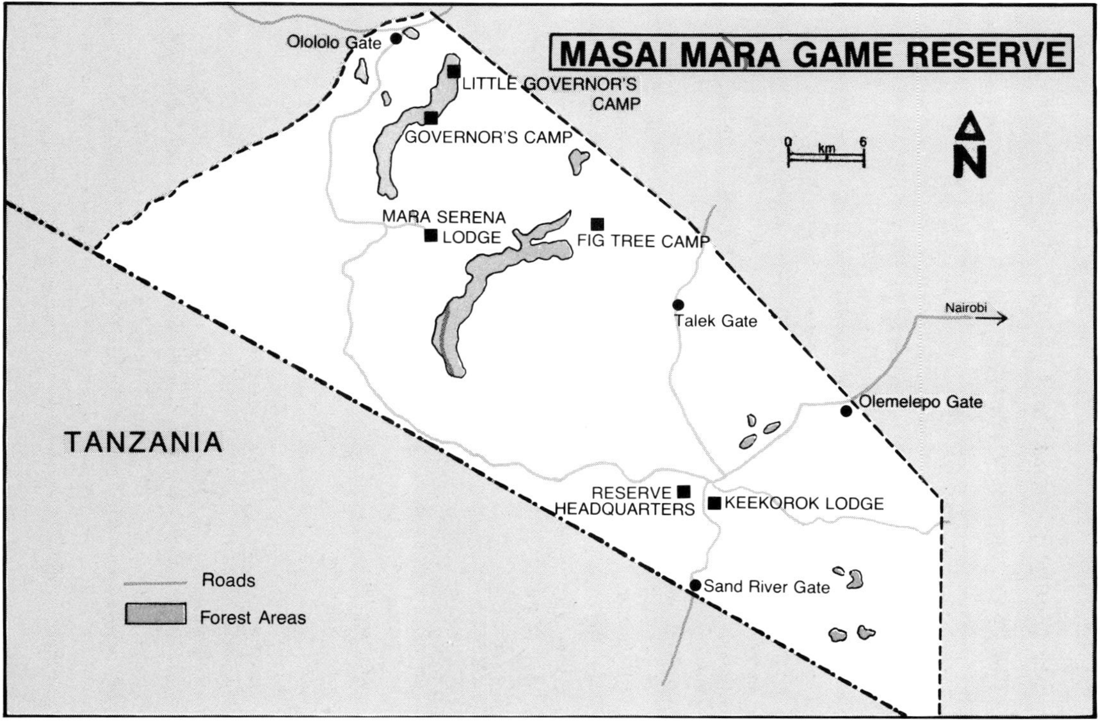
MASAI MARA GAME RESERVE
N
0 km 6
Ololol Gate
LITTLE GOVERNOR'S CAMP
GOVERNOR'S CAMP
MARA SERENA LODGE
FIG TREE CAMP
Talek Gate
Nairobi
Olemelepo Gate
TANZANIA
RESERVE HEADQUARTERS
KEEKOROK LODGE
Sand River Gate
Roads
Forest Areas

Marsabit City is the administrational centre of the region, and has been the place where the nomads from Ethiopia, Somalia and Kenya meet for as long as can be remembered. In this city are additional lodgings. The best and not even the most expensive is the Kenya Lodge.

Transportation: Those who want to travel the route Nairobi — Marsabit by bus, should plan on a two-day trip with one overnight stay in the western town of Isiolo. Catching the bus going to Marsabit in time is a matter of luck. Those who rent a car will reach Marsabit within one day.

Masai Mara National Reserve

Many visitors who have been to several national parks during their stay in Kenya consider "the Mara" located in the very southwest of Kenya to be the most beautiful game reserve in the country. Founded in 1961 and covering an area of 1,800 square kilometres (702 square miles) this park is a uniform ecosystem like the world-famous Serengeti, characterised by hilly grasslands and dark gallery woods. Thanks to the favourable climate and regular rainfall, the Masai Mara has an unusually large stock of wild game. This becomes obvious during the dry season when the animals congregate around the waterholes and riverbeds. The open expanses are ideal to observe the wildlife, making it possible to spot more than 10 different kinds of animals all at once.

The most "prominent" inhabitants of the reserve prefer certain areas and, thus, are relatively easy to detect. The area around the Keekorok Lodge as well as the Musiara Swamps in the northwest are a favoured hunting ground for lions. The Masai Mara has the country's largest lion population. The leopard, a shy loner, lives mainly along the course of the Mara and Talek rivers. Since these animals only hunt by night, and sleep well hidden on higher boughs, visitors will usually not catch a glimpse of them. However, with some luck, pictures can be taken of their slim cousin, the cheetah. The world's fastest — and most elegant — land mammal prefers hunting its prey (gazelles and antelopes) on the open grasslands. What is absolutely certain is that the visitor will spot elephants, the largest land mammals. Still living in herds of impressive size, the elephants gather along the above mentioned rivers during the dry season. Visitor will meet up several smaller groups everywhere in the reserve during the rainy season. Under the strict protection of the rangers, a few rhinoceroses have survived the unchecked poaching up to present in the so-called Rhino Ridge area. The black African buffalo, a very strong animal which is easily irritated, can be seen in more or less large herds everywhere in the reserve. Those who drive in their own car through the reserve

should always keep a safe distance to the herds — many tourists have already been severely injured by charging buffaloes.
When confronted with such a large number of impressive big game, the rest of the animal world may easily be overlooked, although a large population of predators hint at an even larger stock of grazing animals. Various kinds of gazelles, zebras, hyenas and jackals, giraffes and ostriches make the safari into a trip through the past; what the visitors sees is just as the entire country looked when the first Europeans came to Kenya. Every year, a memorable spectacle takes place in the Masai Mara. Hundreds of thousands of gnus gather in the Serengeti to migrate to the north. In July, they reach their destination: the extensive grasslands in the eastern regions of the reserve. When crossing the Mara River, dramatic scenes can be observed: hundreds of gnus stuck in the muddy shore or, unable to climb steep slope on the opposite side, they are trampled to death by the other climbing animals.

Masai Mara National Reserve / **Practical Information**

Accomodation

Keekorok Lodge, c/o P.O. Box 47557 Nairobi, Tel: 335807, £43/£56 ($81/$106). The oldest and still one of the most luxurios lodges in the park.
Mara Serena Lodge, c/o P.O. Box 48690 Nairobi, Tel: 339800, £43/£56 ($81/$106). The largest lodge in the reserve, located in a very beautiful environment. This lodge grants discounts of up to 40% during the low season.
Governor's Camp (with Little Governor's Camp), c/o P.O. Box 48217 Nairobi, Tel: 331871/2. Luxury camp in the bush near the Musiara swamps with a large number of wild animals. All tents are spacious and have a masoned bath and shower to the rear.
The following camps are less expensive than the lodges already mentioned, but are no less attractive.
Fig Tree Camp, P.O. Box 67868 Nairobi, Tel: 21439. This idyllic camp, surrounded on three sides by the Talek River, is only accessible by a small wooden bridge. Generous discounts during low season.
Mara River Camp, P.O. Box 45456 Nairobi, Tel: 21992/3/4. The camp in the northwestern corner of the reserve is an ideal place to start off on safaris to the Musiara Swamp with its large animal population, a paradise for bird-watching.
Apart from the lodgings already mentioned, there are only a few camp sites within the reserve (Crocodile, Fly and Paradise Campsites). These, however, do not have sanitary facilities. There are additional campsites at the main entrances of the reserve (Olemelepo, Sand River, Musiara, Oloolo).

Transportation: Almost all visitors reach the Masai Mara via the little town of Narok, 140 kilometres (87½ miles) southwest of Nairobi. Narok is a centre for the Masai, and the trip here lasts a little over 100 kilometres (62½ miles) on a packed dirt road. Those who are on the road with their own car, should plan in a full day to get to the reserve. No planning is necessary for visitors who rely on one of the numerous safari agencies and book a tour of several days to the Masai Mara *(→Travel in Kenya).*

Medical Care

Hospitals with modern standards can be found in Nairobi and Mombasa. In the tourist centres along the coast, qualified medical care is available through well-educated Indian and European physicians. The rural regions are served by a network of district hospitals, yet their hygienic conditions are often disastrous. Thus, for those travelling extensively around the country, it is advisable to become a member of the "Flying Doctor Emergency Service" (P.O. Box 30125, Nairobi, Tel: 501 301). In emergencies, this service will transport patients by air to Nairobi from any location even in the wilderness. If the patient's condition does not allow transportation, paramedics can even operate on the spot. If one has missed certain phases of the vaccination process for various tropical diseases, these can also be administered in Nairobi and Mombasa *(→Medication).*

Medication

During recent years, the number of Kenya's tourists who died of Malaria has increased to an alarming degree. In fact, adequate prevention of Malaria is more and more difficult because these parasites transmitted by the anopheles mosquito have become increasingly resistant. Fever, dizziness and shivering fits are symptoms of malaria. In general, one starts with the prophylactic treatment three weeks before departing to Kenya. It ends three weeks after having returned home. People often forget that malaria prevention is not a vaccination but a prophylactic treatment. The risk of being bitten cannot be absolutely excluded. The effect can be reduced to a minimum if the pills are taken consistently. In case one's supply of medication is used up, Chloroquine pills (Nivaquin, Paludrin, Aralen, Daraprim, Resochin) are also available in every pharmacy in larger towns. Of course, prevention is not limited to taking pills. It is advisable to use an insect-repellent (Bonomol, Autan) in the evening before going to bed, and also to wear long-sleeve shirts, long trousers and socks. Those who stay at the coast or at Lake Victoria, should definitely use a mosquito net. Mosquito coils are also available everywhere in

Kenya. These are lit below the bed and glow for about 8 hours, filling the room with a mosquito repellant.

In the tropics, open wounds such as bites and scratches do not heal as quickly as they do at home. These can develop into an unpleasant infection; thus, it is definitey advisable to bring along antiseptic ointment.

The reason package tourists who stay in one of the large beach hotels suffer from diarrhoea during their first few days in Kenya, is not the meals but the extensive consumption of ice cubes in soft drinks and alcoholic beverages. Also, the humid tropical climate adds to physical strain, and the direct sun can actually cause severe burns. Therefore, use at least protection factor 15 and wear a hat.

→*Medical Care, Pharmacies, Vaccinations, Clothing and Equipment*

Meru National Park

The Meru National Park has a variety of sights which can hardly be paralleled anywhere else and is one of the least visited parks. Covering 1,554 square kilometres (606 square miles), it is located at the eastern slope of Mount Kenya, about 300 kilometres (187 miles) from Nairobi. Perhaps it is the highest mountain in Kenya, that keeps tourists from visiting this beautiful area. The catchment basin of the Rojewero River to the north is the most beautiful part of the park, with an enormous animal population. Dark gallery forests interspersed with some dum palm groves line the riverbanks, crowded with hordes of apes and innumerous birds. A large herd of elephants has obviously chosen to settle in the swamp area near the Meru Mulika Lodge. Grevy zebras and giraffes, typical for northern Kenya live north of the Rojewero, a landscape of mainly acacias and open grassland. South of the river, the land quite abruptly turns into dry, dusty thorn-bush savanna. This is a favoured habitat of the rare Gerenuk and Kudu antelopes. Meru National Park became world-famous as the home of the lioness Elsa, immortalised by Joy Adamson in her books and the film.

Relatively good trail lead through the park. Unlike other parks, like for example the →*Amboseli National Park,* which have already been developed for tourism, Meru National Park still offers a piece of untouched nature. Visitors must be prepared that they might not see another car during a tour through the park, and that they will remain alone in the wilderness for the entire day. Given the circumstances, visitors are assigned a ranger at the park entrance to accompany them.

Meru National Park / **Practical Information**

Accomodation

Meru Mulika Lodge, c/o P.O. Box 42013 Nairobi, Tel: 29751/23488/330820, £23/£33 ($43/$62). Located directly at the swamp with its large numbers of game, this lodge is only 5 kilometres (about 3 miles) from the Murera Gate. Visitors coming from Nairobi or one of the other heavily frequented national parks will very much enjoy the lodge's idyllic location and the very friendly staff.

Leopard Rock Self Service Bandas, reservations can be booked through A.A. Travel Limited, P.O. Box 14982 Nairobi, Tel: 7429 26. Well-tended grounds with simple self-catering huts, electricity and water.

There are campsites near the park administration office.

Mombasa

Mombasa is the second largest city of Kenya; its harbour Kilindini is — after Durban/South Africa — the second largest harbour on the African continent. It is the final destination of the Mombasa Highway coming from Nairobi as well of the East African railway. More than 50 mosques and a number of Hindu and Sikh temples render a Middle Eastern flair to this city — a city with a history spanning almost 2,000 years. Quite different from the bustling character of Nairobi, the atmosphere of Mombasa is rather complacent and laid-back, perhaps a concession to the steamy climate. The centre of the city is situated on an island, four-fifths of which is surrounded by the mainland. At the southern tip of the island is the Old Town which is still the heartbeat of Mombasa, consisting of narrow streets and alleyways, small squares and the famous Fort Jesus. In the faces of the residents (who often wear the traditional Arabian robes), one can trace the colourful history of this city: Arabs, Persian and Indians have all had their infuence.

There were already settlements on Mombasa Island even before the Arabs arrived. The island was mentioned for the first time in the famous "Periplus of the Eritrean Sea," a handbook for seafarers written by a Greek merchant in the 1st century A.D. The chronicle of Kilwa, written in the 12th century A.D. as well as Arabian travellers reported of a town with four-storey stone buildings called "Al Mambasi" in the Middle Ages. Ten thousand people of African-Arabian origin lived in this city upon the arrival of Vasco da Gama, the Portuguese seafarer. Da Gama on his way to India, was brusquely denied entry when he knocked at the gates of the city in 1498 — the people had already learned of the clash between the Portuguese and the Arabian merchants in Mozambique. In 1505, 1528 and 1589 ensuing Portuguese expeditions avenged the inhospitable welcome da Gama

received by looting and destroying Mombasa. An unsuccessful military campaign against →*Malindi* (a Portuguese ally) finally put an end to the city-state's independence: in 1593, the Portuguese erected the mighty Fort Jesus on the eastern end of Mombasa Island, which still has its original impressive appearance today. Its function was to guard access to the harbour and to stall the native Swahili population who were only superficially under control. The power and the commercial monopoly were always unstable since Lisbon was far away, and supplies had to be shipped over long distances. After several wars, the troops of the Sultan of Oman conquered the Fort in 1698, after having besieged it for three years. Every single man in the Portuguese garrison was killed. Under the Mazrui dynasty (originating from Oman) who proclaimed independence from the sultan shortly after takeing power, Mombasa was to see another economic and cultural peak. The Arabian elite determined the fate of the city, in consultation with the native Swahilis. It was only in 1837 that Oman could retake the city and strengthen his rule. In 1840, the sultan moved his court to Sansibar, from where he continued ruling his possessions in East Africa. Towards the middle of the 19th century, Mombasa, like Sansibar, became the centre of the slave and ivory trade in East Africa and served as a base for numerous European discoverers and research expeditions on their way into the country's interior. In 1846, the German missionaries Rebmann and Krapf founded the first missionary station of East Africa on the mainland in Rabai, opposite Mombasa.
British ships had already been sailing off the coast since the 1920's, when in 1895 the British made Mombasa the administration headquarters of the "British East African Protectorate," this until 1907. The British then moved the colonial administration to Nairobi, and the port lost importance. However, with the new deep sea port of Kilindini it regained its predominant role in this area. Mombasa is an crutial gateway to the world market for its neighbours Uganda, Ruanda and Burundi, which do not have an access to the ocean themselves.

Mombasa / **Sights**

Fort Jesus

When tourists visit Mombasa, they start their trip through the old city from the massive fortress with its 16 metre (53 feet) high and 2.5 metre (8 feet) thick walls. Two canons to the right of the entrance, originate from battle ships from World War I, emphasising the embattlement atmosphere of the fortress. Built between 1591 and 1593 by an Italian architect, craftspeople from Goa and African workers according to the latest military-strategical knowledge, it was thought to be impenetrable for a long time. Its five ramparts were built in such a way that dead

PORT TUDOR
Nyali Bridge
Abdel
Tom Mboya Avenue
Tom Mboya Avenue
Ronald Ngara Road
Salim Mwa Ngunga Rd.
Makupa Bridge
Jomo Kenyatta Avenue
Biash
Lumumba Road
6
Haile Se
Kisum
11
Moi Avenu
to the Airport
INDUSTRIAL AREA
KILINDINI
PORT REITZ

MOMBASA ISLAND

Legende:

1. Fort Jesus Museum
2. Bohra Mosque
3. Old Bridge (no longer in use)
4. Market
5. Post Office
6. Makupa Market
7. British Council
8. Tusks (the symbol of Mombasa)
9. Mbaraki Column
10. YMCA
11. Tourist Information Office
12. Likoni Ferry

angles were avoided, making attacking forces more easily combatted. Through the main gate, on which a bronze plaque briefly outlines the turbulent history of this fortress, one is led up a murky path to a surprisingly spacious inner courtyard. Diagonally opposite to the entrance, a museum (open daily from 8:30 am to 6 pm) has been set up in the former soldiers' quarters, displaying interesting items from the Swahili culture and pictures of the salvage work of the Portuguese frigate "Santa Antonio de Tanna," which sank at the entrance of the harbour.
In 1697, the ship was sent to provide the garrison of the fort under attack with food and soldiers, but before it could reach the harbour it was sunk by the Omani canons — right before the eyes of the desperate Portuguese. The collection is complemented by Indian and Persian ceramics and shards of porcelain originating from China. A walk along the battlements offers a good impression of the dimensions of the fort and — looking over the parapet down to the Arabian old town — the feeling of estrangement and isolation can be perceived, which many Portuguese soldiers certainly must have felt occasionally. The most interesting view is from the sea-side of the fortress. Between the two bastion towers *San Matias* and *San Mateus* is the commander's house as well as an arcade leading to the outside walls of the fort. The so-called *Omani-House,* a massive watch-tower located to the right of the entrance, was built on the ruins of the *San Felipe* bastion and has been completely restored. From the top, one can enjoy a wonderful panorama, overlooking the mosques and the temples of old Mombasa. One can then follow the small path to the left of the entrance, leading down to the sea. From here, the outer walls of the fort with the coat of arms of two Portuguese kings can be seen hanging at the two bastions. Up to 1958, the Fort Jesus was used as a prison by the British; in 1960, it was declared a national monument.

The Old Town of Mombasa

The old town begins to the left of Fort Jesus. On the way to the fort one will pass *Treasury Square,* surrounded by administration buildings built in the typical British colonial style. Originally, the Uganda railway ended at this point.
The *Old Town* is not as old as one might think at first sight. The constant humidity badly damages the beautiful buildings, as one can easily see. Unfortunately, there is no money available for their restoration and maintenance. Most of the buildings were built during the 19th century, although the foundations and portions of the walls are much older. The layout of the old town is similar to other Swahili towns along the coast. It is a confused labyrinth of narrow streets and alleyways, which either end in courtyards or at small squares. The people living in the old town use these as assembly places to discuss residential issues. This scene is

dominated by the impressive, multi-storeyed stone houses of the established families of Arabian and Asian descent. These houses were built in the so-called *Sansibar style.* The facades are decorated with hand-carved verandas and small, barred windows. In earlier times, the owners of the houses resided with their families in the upper storeys, while the slaves were quartered on the dank ground floor.

Coming from the Fort Jesus, one enters the old town by way of the main street, the ''ndia kuu.'' To the right side, one will discover ''Ali's Curio Shop,'' a souvenir shop which beats the drum a little too insistently for its products, in a number of languages. The first British police station was set up in this building, which was built around 1900. The oldest mosque in town is the *Mandhry-Mosque* on Bachawy Road. It was built around 1570 by the Mandhry family, who still lives in Mombasa. Its clumsy, slightly tilted minaret can be seen all the way from the Fort Jesus. One is only allowed to climb the tower after prior consultation with the local religious leaders. Its interior is whitewashed and quite sober. To the north side is the prayer corner, facing Mecca. Prior to entering this mosque — as is the case with every other mosque in Kenya — one should ask permission and follow the clothing etiquette: men should wear long trousers; women, knee-length skirts and blouses which cover the shoulders. Behind the mosque, several pathways descend to the old *Government Square.* Formerly, this place was the undisputed centre of the town. This is where the old customs house, shops selling valuable carpets and the fish market with its penetrating smell are located. With a little luck, one may see one of the Arabian sailing ships when standing at the gate leading to the entrance of the harbour. The great age of the Jahazis, Booms and Sambuks finally came to an end with the diesel engine. One should be cautious: although it sounds strange, it is prohibited to take pictures of the harbour facilities. Policemen wearing sun-glasses patrol this area, but, from what one hears, they can be sometimes be persuaded to allow this. The Asian temples are located at the edge of the old town, mostly hidden from the street by facades of houses. The most beautiful of these exotic temples is without a doubt the *Jain Temple* on Langoni Road. It is built almost entirely out of white marble. This is the religious centre of the Jain Hindus. Though the followers of the Jain religion (mostly merchants and craftsmen) have a lot in common with the Indian Hindus, they reject the caste system. The temple was completed in 1963, and is open to the public. Do not forget to remove your shoes before entering the temple. The noisy Digo Road, marking the beginning of the modern districts of Mombasa begins directly behind the temple. The *Mwembe Tayari Market,* the largest weekly market on the coast takes place here. Only 100 years ago, this market was the base for Arabian and Swahili caravans transporting slaves into the country's interior. Numerous European expeditions started from here, as well. Today, merchants offer an enormous selection of fresh fruit and vegetables, exotic spices and even live animals.

Mombasa / **Practical Information**

Accomodation

The Manor Hotel, Nyerere Avenue, P.O. Box 84851, Tel: 21821, £9/£16 ($17/$29). Built in the 1920's, this is the oldest European hotel in Mombasa and was recently renovated.

Castle Hotel, Moi Avenue, P.O. Box 84231, Tel: 23403/21683/312296, £15/£23 ($28/$43). This is the most widely known hotel among tourists and a popular place to meet.

Glory Guest House, Kwa Shibu Road corner of Chember Road, P.O. Box 85527, Tel: 314557, £5/£7.30 ($9.50/$13.50). This new guest house is run by Glory Car Hire. Guests who rent a car from this agency, redeive a discount.

Lotus Hotel, Mvita Road corner of Cathedral Road, P.O. Box 90193, Tel: 3213207, £8/£12 ($15.50/$22). A hotel with atmosphere from the colonial period.

Banks: Barclay's Bank, Moi Avenue, open Monday to Saturday from 8:30 am to 12:30 pm and 2 to 4:30 pm.

Beaches: Mombasa has no beaches suited to swimming. The fantastic beaches outside the city can be reached with the inexpensive taxis. A larger taxi stand is located in front of the Castle Hotel on Moi Avenue. The beaches near Mombasa are Shelly Beach to the south and Nyali Beach to the north. The Nyali Beach is very popular among the city's residents, since it is much larger than the quiet, but quite narrow Shelly Beach. The recreational facilities can be used for a small fee.

Car Rental: Glory Car Hire, Trans Ocean House, Moi Avenue, P.O. Box 85527, Tel: 21159/313561/493179.

Lofty Safaris, Hassanali Building, Nkrumah Building, Tel: 20241.

Excursions

Mombasa serves as a base for a wide range of interesting day trips to its outskirts. *Bombolulu:* Bombolulu is a training centre for the physically handicapped people, and is located 4 kilometres (2½ miles) north of Mombasa. Meanwhile, more than 180 men and women are kept occupied in a workshop and in the neighbouring gardens. Costume jewellry, necklaces and bracelets made from colonial coins are produced here. Young people from all over Kenya absolve their two-year training and further education programmes in Bombolulu, in order to become acquainted with the new agricultural methods (open Monday to Saturday from 8 am to 6 pm,

Tel: 471704). After Bombolulu one leaves Mombasa via the Nyali Bridge. A few miles beyond Bombolulu is the *Bamburi Nature Trail,* a piece of "repaired" nature. The land was purchased from the cement plants nearby at the end of the 1960's. The newly planted trees and some fish ponds have attracted numerous kinds of birds (among others cranes, pelicans) which can be observed up close.

Krapf Memorial and *Freretown:* A visit to these two historical sites is a good way of concluding one's tour through the old city of Mombasa. Leaving Mombasa via the Nyali Bridge heading toward Malindi, the turn-off to the Krapf Memorial is shortly beyond the bridge. The memorial in memory of the German missionary Johann Ludwig Krapf is perched atop a knoll. Working for the English Church Missionary Society, he came to East Africa in 1844 to convert the heathens, but was just as unsuccessful as his Portuguese predecessors. After his wife and his child died of malaria shortly after their arrival (their graves are located nearby), Johann Rebmann founded East Africa's first missionary station in Rabai in 1846. One year later, he was the first European to see the snow-covered summit of Mount Kenya during his expedition into the interior of the country. Beyond the memorial, one will cross the extensive exhibition grounds, until one reaches the rocky cliffs of *Mackenzie Point.* During clear weather, one has a very beautiful view of the seaside and the old town of Mombasa on the opposite shore.

→*Shimba Hills National Reserve*

Medical Care: Three hospitals in Mombasa are recommanded: the Aga Khan Hospital (Tel: 312953), the Coast General Hospital (Tel: 24111) and the Katherine Bibby Hospital (Tel: 312190). The international hotels of the city have excellent medical emergency service.

Night Life: After nightfall, the centre of the city becomes deserted. One should take a taxi for longer distances.

Starting from the Castle Hotel the following discotheques can be reached on foot: the Sunshine further down Moi Avenue, the Kasbah on Digo Road and the Birds behind the General Post Office. These dance cafés are frequented by Africans as well as Asian and European guests. The Toyz on Baluchi Street has recently opened.

Postal Service: The General Post Office is located on Digo Road. Open Monday to Friday from 8 am to 4:30 pm, Saturday from 8 am to noon.

Restaurants

Manor Hotel, Nyerere Avenue. This restaurant, housed in Mombasa's oldest hotel, offers a variety of dishes, served in a stylish atmosphere.

Castle Hotel, Moi Avenue. International cuisine with tropical accents dominate the menu of this hotel restaurant. Half of Mombasa meets on the terrace. It is less noisy at the Garden Bar behind the hotel.

Indian Restaurants: Tamarind, Tel: 471747. The best restaurant for seafood in the city. It is best reached best by leaving Mombasa via the Nyali Bridge, turning right after the first traffic light, then following the signs.

Splendid View Restaurant, opposite to Hotel Splendid (see above).

Geetanjali's, Msanifu Kombo Street, Tel: 26260. Simple restaurant with a pleasant atmosphere and local clientele.

Swahili Restaurants: Swahili Curry Bowl, Tangana Road corner of Moi Avenue, Tel: 311084. Traditional Swahili dishes prepared with coconut milk. Open Monday to Saturday from 8 to 10 am, 11 am to 3 pm and 7 to 10 pm

Shopping: The large market halls of Mwembe Tayari are located between Digo Road and Biashara Street. Eloquent merchants from all over the country sing the praises a wide selection of tropical fruit. Behind the halls, are the spice shops run by Indian merchants.

A large selection of sisal bags, wood and soapstone carvings among other articles can be found around the traffic circle of Moi Avenue and Digo Road.

Transportation: Cross-country buses and long-distance taxis, the railway and the airlines connect Mombasa with the other parts of Kenya. The Akamba, Goldline and Coast Buses offer departures to Nairobi, starting at the bus station on Jomo Kenyatta Avenue corner of Mwembe Tayari. Here, one can also find a ticket office. Buses to Malinda and Lamu operate several times daily from the Abdel Nasser Road. The best and most comfortable way to travel to Nairobi is to use the Kenya Railways. Two night trains (leaving at 5 pm and 7 pm) offer comfortable sleeper cars departing daily from Mombasa and arriving in Nairobi at 8 am and 8:30 am. Only recently, a train was set up especially for tourists to take this on this beautiful route during the daytime. Tickets are available at the train station or at travel agencies; reservations should be made several days in advance. Kenya Airways serves the route Mombasa-Nairobi several times daily. Smaller charter airlines, for example Cooper Skybird or Equator Airlines, take passengers to Malindi and Lamu. Tickets are available at the airport or travel agencies.

Travel Agencies: Among the numerous travel agencies along the Moi Avenue, the Faraways Safari Centre (P.O. Box 87815, Tel: 23307/9) is especially worth recommending. Located opposite the Castle Hotel, this agency arranges flights and tours by train as well as hotel reservations.

Money

the unit of currency is the Kenya-Shilling (KSH). It is based on the decimal system. The following denominations of banknotes are in circulation: 10, 20, 50, 100, 200 and 500 KSH. Coin denominations are 5, 10, 20 and 50 cents, as well as 1 and 5 KSH. The exchange rate was £1:6KSH and $1:26KSH in the summer of 1991. Cash and traveller's cheques can be exchanged at all banks and in the tourist hotels (at a less favourable exchange rate).

Business hours for banks: Monday to Friday from 8:30 am to 1 pm, Saturday 8:30 to 11 am. Tourists prefer traveller's cheques (for example American Express, Visa) These are much safer than cash since they can be replaced if by lost or stolen at every authorized office by presenting the receipt of purchase.

Credit cards (American Express, Master Card, or EuroCard) are accepted in places frequented by tourists. The advantage of credit cards is to be able to pay without cash (hotel bills, rental cars and air tickets), and to enjoy insurance coverage, if flights or rental car is paid by credit card.

→*Currency*

Nairobi

No one who travels through Kenya, will be able to avoid a stay in Nairobi: all roads, rails and flight routes lead to this, the biggest, most progressive metropolis in East Africa. Located 120 kilometres (75 miles) south of the equator, and 1,800 metres (5,886 feet) above sea level, Nairobi derives its name from the KiMaa language of the Masai, and means ''cold swamp.'' The highlands which were often overcast was not considered a very inviting place by the natives whose herds of cattle grazed in the area only 90 years ago.

Today's Nairobi of makes a greater fuss over its visitors' well-being. Probably no other African city offers such a wide range of accommodations and restaurants. At no other place on the continent — apart from South Africa — are there so many shops, book stores, cinemas, clubs and car rental agencies. Kenya's capital is the unquestioned economic and cultural centre of East Africa and the seat of numerous UN organizations.

Some of the visitors — and even more of the residents — having made their own experiences prefer to call Nairobi ''Nairobbery.'' Even within the well-tended, representative city, the enormous social differences have become a visible fact of life. Nairobi is a city of superlatives, but some of these are better left unmentioned by the city elders: Nairobi is one of the fastest growing cities in Africa. More than half of its residents are inconceivably poor. These people live under inhumane

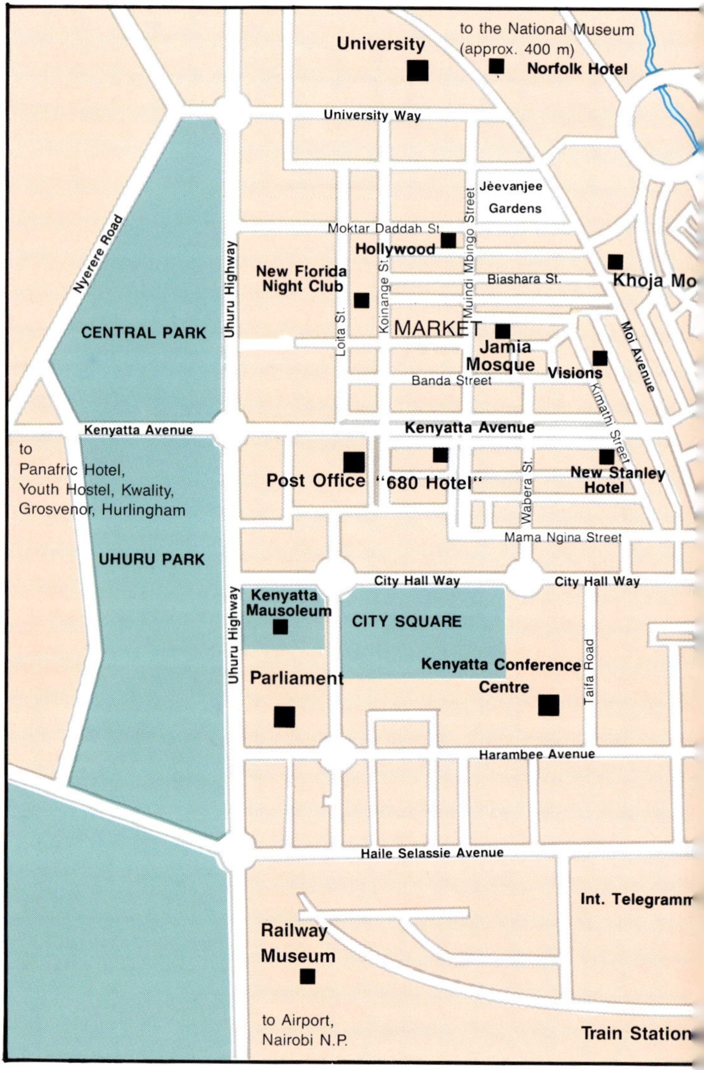
University
to the National Museum
(approx. 400 m)
Norfolk Hotel
University Way
Jèevanjee
Gardens
Moktar Daddah St.
Hollywood
Muindi Mbingo Street
Nyerere Road
Uhuru Highway
New Florida
Night Club
Koinange St.
Biashara St.
Khoja Mo
Loita St.
MARKET
CENTRAL PARK
Jamia
Mosque
Moi Avenue
Visions
Banda Street
Kimathi Street
Kenyatta Avenue
Kenyatta Avenue
to
Panafric Hotel,
Youth Hostel, Kwality,
Grosvenor, Hurlingham
Post Office
"680 Hotel"
Wabera St.
New Stanley
Hotel
Mama Ngina Street
UHURU PARK
City Hall Way
City Hall Way
Kenyatta
Mausoleum
CITY SQUARE
Uhuru Highway
Kenyatta Conference
Centre
Taifa Road
Parliament
Harambee Avenue
Haile Selassie Avenue
Int. Telegramm
Railway
Museum
to Airport,
Nairobi N.P.
Train Station

CENTRAL NAIROBI
N
0
250 m
Nairobi River
Kirinyaga Road
River Road
ccra Road
Cross Road
li Road
River Road
Racecourse Road
Pumwani
Road
Ronald Ngala Road
KBS BUS
STATION
MARKETPLACE
Nairobi
River
MARKET
Ring
ssie Avenue
COUNTRY
BUS
TERMINAL

conditions in slums without electricity or running water, only 10 minutes by car from the Nairobi Hilton. Many of them opt for the direct method of "earning" money — a development which becomes visible in the form of barred shop windows and heavily armed guards standing in front of the bank buildings. Theft and fraud are part of the daily life in the centre of the city. Thus, it is advisable to pay special attention to valuables as well as to keep a watchful eye on the people passing by. In general, people view the city differently. Those who do not only want to take pictures of wild animals, but want to get to know more of an African country with modern standards, will find what they seek in Nairobi. The city hums with activity both day and night. On the streets, one meets people from all parts of the country as well as from Asia and Europe — an ethnic variety that one can hardly find anywhere else. Those who experience the vibrant city as intensely as the lions and elephants outside the city in the bush, will bring home a wealth of unforgetable impressions.

Nairobi / **History**

Nairobi is barely one hundred years old. In 1897, Sergeant George Ellis drove milestone 327 of the Uganda Railway from Mombasa into the soft ground, not far from where the train station stands today. Indian coolies set up a supply camp of tents and shacks, which were replaced by solid wood and stone houses after only a few years. In 1907, Nairobi took the place of Mombasa as the administrative headquarters of the East African Protectorate. Attracted by publicity campaigns at home, many hundreds of British and white South African settlers started a new life in Nairobi and in the fertile highlands. Aristocrats, millionaires and politicians went on big game hunts under the guidance of experienced scouts. This usually ended in an evening of jovial drinking in the Norfolk Hotel. Among the settlers, moral standards were rather low. The protectorate soon gained the reputation of an stylish country club of sorts, and in England, conversations often started with a cynical "are you married or do you live in Kenya?" The great Kenyan authors Beryl Markham, Elspeth Huxley and Karen Blixen *(→Literature)* left impressive portrayals of this period. In 1931, this protectorate was raised to the status of Kenya Colony, which was in the same year as Karen Blixen was forced to give up her coffee plantation located at the base of the Ngong Hills. Meanwhile, 40,000 people lived in the capital; 7000 were Europeans, whose leader, Lord Delamere, forced London to grant the white settlers their own national assembly. During World War II, Nairobi was a garrison town, a base from which a British expedition corps conquered Ethiopia, then occupied by Italian troops.

Africans and Indians were not allowed to own land. Thus, the Africans went to Nairobi and were forced into unskilled labour to earn enough to pay their taxes — the tax rates differed from those paid by whites. After their contracts as railway workers had either expired or had been revoked, the Indians stayed in Nairobi and made their living as wholesalers or as clerks in retail shops. Because racial segregation was common practice, the European residential areas were set up separately from the African or Indian quarters, as can still be seen today. The eastern districts of Kariokor, Starehe, Pumwani, Eastleigh and Kaloleni are still the traditional residential areas for underpriviledged Africans. The squalid dwellings in Mathare Valley have grown into one of the largest slums in Africa. To the southwest are Jamhuri, Kilimani and Woodley, comfortable residential areas for Europeans and wealthy Asians and Africans. Located above the city on the northern hills, the Westlands, the Parklands, and above all, the embassy area Muthaiga, with its golf corses and luxury shopping centres make visitors forget for a moment, that Kenya is a third-world country.

Nairobi / **Sights**

The city of Nairobi presents itself as a clearly structured square which can easily be encountered on foot. Forming its borders are *Haile Selassie Avenue* to the south, the *Uhuru Highway* to the west and *Moi Avenue* to the east. The old centre of the city with its buildings partly dating from the colonial time is located beyond Moi Avenue.

After having arrived in Nairobi, the best place to visit first is the *National Museum* (P.O. Box 406558, Tel: 742161, open daily from 9:30 am to 6 pm, bus line 23 from the Hilton). This museum was founded in 1910 and is located 2 kilometres (1¼ miles) outside the city on Museum Hill. Objects from the culture of most ethnic groups of Kenya (unfortunately not very well arranged), as well as prehistoric finds, an exhibition on the Swahili culture and paintings by Joy Adamson offer an overview of Kenya's cultural heritage. A gigantic, fibreglass sculpture by Ahmed, supposedly the biggest elephant to have wandered the landscapes of Kenya *(→Marsabit National Park)* is set up in the inner courtyard. Opposite the entrance is the *Snake Park* which is, to put it mildly, a little run-down, and only worth visiting for snake fans.

Not far from the National Museum, is the world-famous *Norfolk Hotel* which had an established reputation long before the film "Out of Africa" was presented. It was opened on December 25, 1904 and is the oldest hotel in Nairobi. Today, one can hardly imagine that in earlier times the wilderness started right behind the building. By night, armed guards had to ward off lions and leopards from the hotel's kitchen. Most of the settlers coming to the Norfolk were aristocrats, so that the hotel was given the epithet of ''House of Lords.'' In the bar (today: *Delamere Bar*), grass-roots politics were made and less patriotic speeches held, since many guests dreamed of an independent, white Kenya, similar to South Africa. Spirits peaked, and conversation waned, when such famous drinkers as Lord Delamere *(→History)* or the authors Ernest Hemingway and Robert Ruark ensured a lively atmosphere. Today's Norfolk is doubtlessly less noisy, but it is still the top hotel in the city. It should by all means be chosen over the other, modern luxury hotels in Nairobi. The *Delamere Terrace* on Harry Thuku Road opens to the street, inviting visitors to stop for coffee and cake. The restaurant is one of the best on the African continent. Those who are interested in the colonial period, can have a look at the rickshaw and horse-drawn carriages ''Bwana'' and ''Memsahib'' in the inner courtyard.

The *City Market* is locatedon Muindi Mbingu Street, a five-minute-walk south of the Norfolk. In contrast to the nostalgic atmosphere and the colonial romanticism of the Norfolk, one now can experience the colourful, vibrant and modern Kenya of today. The market is housed in a former hangar. All types of fruit and vegetables which grow in East Africa, are sold here throughout the year. In the galleries on the upper floor, a large supply of hand-made souvenirs await the visitor. However, it is no less expensive here than anywhere else, and the merchants do not like to bargain. Diagonally across from the market, the silver dome of the *Jamia Mosque* towers into the sky. The Mogul style served as a model when this mosque was built between 1925 and 1933. It is subsidised by Saudi Arabia and the affluent Islamic congregation of Nairobi. Visitors are only allowed to enter this, the largest Islamic building in East Africa if they remove their shoes and observe the strict regulations regarding clothing. The sublime quiet of the interior embraces the visitor — a drastic contrast to the hectic streets outside. The other large mosque in Nairobi is the *Khoja Mosque* in the Moi Avenue, located on the corner of Biashara Street. It is not easily recognised from the street. The mosque is the spiritual centre for the Israelites, a progressive Islamic denomination under the leadership of Aga Khan. At its lower end, the Muindi Mbingu Street leads to the prestigious avenue of Nairobi, the Kenyatta Avenue. This is the city's main artery. The founders of the city had already laid this street out so generously that a cart drawn by 12 oxen could easily make a full turn. One can almost say that the Kenyatta Avenue was conceived, before the city itself was founded. Today, the most beautiful shops and boutiques, some of the best hotels as well as banks and office buildings line this avenue. The service of one of the numerous shoe cleaners should only be accepted after a careful inspection of the supplies used — it is very likely that in

the heat of the moment one's shoes are not polished but ruined. Just as the city's chronicle is inconceivable without the Norfolk Hotel, the *New Stanley Hotel* is just as historically interesting. It was founded in 1917, and its interior is reminiscent of the ''good old colonial times.'' Just as popular among tourists and globetrotters is the *Thorn Tree Cafe* which belongs to the hotel — this street cafe enjoys an almost legendary reputation. In colonial times, it was laid out around a thorn tree which has grown dramatically in the meantime. Farmers and hunters used this thorn tree as a bulletin board by pinning up messages for friends and relatives on its bark. This custom is still alive and well and makes the Thorn Tree Cafe the inofficial communications centre in Nairobi. Today the cafe's management has put up real bulletin boards to protect the tree. Those who looking for company on a safari to the national parks or just want to meet with someone, can simply leave a message on the board. It is surprising how well this system works.
A 15-minute-walk from the Thorn Tree Cafe, one arrives at the *Railway Museum* (open daily from 8:30 am to 4:45 pm, Saturday to 3:30 pm, closed Sundays). It

Kenyatta Avenue is the main traffic artery of Nairobi

is located near the train station at the end of Station Road. On exhibit are historical photographs of the times when the Uganda railway was under construction, as well as old steam engines and wagons. Some of these were used in filming "Out of Africa" after having been carefully polished.

The government and administration buildings are located between Haile Selassie Avenue, Uhuru Highway, City Hall Way and Moi Avenue. Their dreary, modern facades are similar to the architecture of official buildings in many other countries. Only the *Parliament* on the Parliament Road at the corner of Harambee Avenue is worth a second glance. The northern part of the building dates from the colonial time, whereas the construction of the southern part was first completed in 1965. Magnificent mosaics, frescoes and African sculptures decorate the lobby and the stairways leading to the assembly hall. It is possible to visit an open plenary session, provided one first registers at the reception. While the Thorn Tree Cafe is the inofficial centre of the city, the *Kenyatta Conference Centre* is the official symbol of Nairobi. Located between the Harambee Avenue and City Square, it was built between 1964 and 1973. The impressive tower is the seat of the ruling party KANU, with a rotating restaurant on the 28th floor. When the weather is clear, the restaurant or the observation platform above offer a memorable view of the Ngong Hills and the yellow expanses of the Masai savanna. The shape of the wings next to the tower is meant to reflect traditional African architecture. The gigantic room inside the building can seat more than 700 conference participants. Located in front of the Conference Centre, the *City Square* is dominated by the monumental statue of Jomo Kenyatta, the first president of the Kenyan Republic. The Supreme Court can be seen behind the statue. It was built in the neoclassical style and dates back to the colonial time. The old, great man's eyes look to the *Kenyatta Mausoleum* which is located a few hundred metres farther. On August 22, 1978, the deceased statesman was laid to rest here. The mausoleum is not open to the public — photography is also prohibited.

As soon as visitors cross Moi Avenue in the eastern districts of Nairobi, they will have the impression of having entered a different world. Suddenly, the faceless modern multi-storeyed buildings give way to the street bazaars and the colourful two-storeyed office buildings of the Asian business people, which are on the verge of dilapidation. When Nairobi was a young city, this was its centre, and there are still even some of the traditional, covered sidewalks. This part of the city is not at all as dangerous as it may seem when looking at the numerous rag-tag figures and smelling these strange odours. Globetrotters from all over the world stay here at one of the less expensive hotels, and enjoy the local food in one of the numerous restaurants. The Indian shops on the Biashara Street sell everything from exotic spices, metal suitcases and music cassettes to batik clothes and diving goggles. Most local bus companies have settled into this part of the city, and this is also where most of the long-distance taxis start on their trips to all parts of the country. Since this part of the city bustles around the clock and is always teeming with people, it is much safer to walk around here at night than in the city which may seem deserted at that time, but just might not be.

Nairobi / **Sights near the City**

Bomas of Kenya (Forest Edge Road, P.O. Box 40689, Tel: 891801, open Monday to Friday from 9 am to 5 pm, Saturday and Sunday from 1 pm to 6 pm, bus line 24 from Development House, Moi Avenue). Located on the outskirts of Nairobi, this open-air-museum has a spacious auditorium seating up to 200 spectators, where professional dance groups perform traditional dances and songs daily at 2:30 pm. Next to it, a model village was built, showing examples of pre-European architecture and typical Kenyan farms. The Bomas of Kenya are located on Ngong Road (later: Langata Road) 10 kilometres (6¼ miles) outside of Nairobi and is accessible by car.

Karen Blixen Museum (Karen Road, located in a suburb with the same name, open daily from 9:30 am to 6 pm, bus line 24 from the Nairobi Hilton).

The Danish baroness Karen Blixen who once set off to found a farm in Kenya, has became very famous since the filming of her novel "Out of Africa." Her biography is famous throughout the world: in 1914, she arrived with her husband Bror Blixen in Kenya, and bought a coffee farm at the base of the picturesque Ngong Hills. After a short while, the couple separated by mutual consent, and Karen Blixen fell deeply in love with the English adventurer Denys Finch-Hatton. After a few wonderful years, he died in an accident, and the farm fell victim to the world economic crisis. In 1931, Blixen finally returned to Denmark.

In Kenya, there was a prompt reaction to the Blixen boom: in spring 1968, their residential building was converted into a museum and an initiative was founded to buy back all of the original furnishings, then dispersed throughout the world. Now, Karen fans from all over the world inspect the cuckoo clock above the fireplace, the Finch-Hatton bookcase and of course the enchanting bedroom. In the garden, the old coffee roasting house was restored according to the original plans.

Nairobi National Park (open daily from 6:15 am to 6 pm)

Not rare animals, but the mere existence of this national park is the real attraction. The park covers an area of 114 square kilometres (44 square miles) and is a patch of unspoiled African wilderness, which can be seen from the Kenyatta

Conference Centre. It offers a habitat not only to elephants, but also to more than 70 kinds of mammals, for example lions, giraffes and buffaloes. A high fence keeps the animals from straying into the city or onto the Mombasa Highway; yet, it is open to the south to allow the savanna animals to roam freely. For those who did not plan a safari tour to one of the famous game reserves, the Nairobi National Park offers the opportunity to observe big game against the backdrop of a beautiful landscape during a half-day trip. There is a network of roads with many signs leading visitors through the park. It is passable for normal cars. At the park's entrance, information is available where certain kinds of animals can be most easily spotted. The highest concentration of game is in the western part of the park. *Impala Hill* is a popular destination for tours, and is also the highest point in the park, offering a beautiful panorama when weather is clear. A small colony of hippopotamuses lives on the moist banks of the *Mbagathi River* in the eastern portion of the park. Other areas such as *Lion Corner* or *Leopard Cliff* do not guarantee that one will see one of these species.

The idyllic village is losing its traditional roots as the younger generations move to the cities of Mombasa and Nairobi

The best time to observe animals is during the ''game drive'' in the early morning or the late afternoon. It is worthwhile to rent a car to visit the park. However, half-day sightseeing tours are also offered by most safari agencies. The Uhuru Highway to Mombasa leads directly from Nairobi to the main entrance. Beyond the stadium, one must turn right onto Langata Road. From here, one can easily follow the signs to Nairobi National Park.

Ngong Racecourse: This is a relic of the ''good old days'' and is still a favourite meeting place for white Kenyans. Every Sunday afternoon horse races take place on the turf located 8 kilometres (5 miles) outside of Nairobi. Buses depart from the Nairobi Hilton to Ngong.

Nairobi / **Practical Information**

Accomodation

In general, it is quite easy to find a hotel in Nairobi. However, it may become difficult when city hosts one or several international conferences.

Hilton International Hotel, Watalii Street, P.O. Box 30624 Nairobi, Tel: 334000, £36.50/£46.50 ($68.50/$87.50)

Nairobi Serena Hotel, Nyerere Road, corner of Kenyatta Avenue, P.O. Box 46302 Nairobi, Tel: 725111, £43/£55 ($81/$103).

New Stanley Hotel, Kenyatta Avenue corner of Kimathi Street, P.O. Box 30680 Nairobi, Tel: 333233, £31/£38 ($58.50/$71).

Norfolk Hotel, Harry Thuku Road, P.O. Box 40064 Nairobi, Tel: 335422, £42.50/£55 ($80/$103).

680 Hotel, Kenyatta Avenue corner of Muindi Mbingu Street, P.O. Box 43436 Nairobi, Tel: 332680, £16/£23 ($30/$43.50).

Oakwood Hotel, Kimathi Street, P.O. Box 40683 Nairobi, Tel: 20592/3, £14/£17.50 ($27/$33).

Hotel Ambassadeur, Moi Avenue, P.O. Box 30399 Nairobi, Tel: 336803, £14/£18 ($27/$33.50).

Milimani Hotel, Milimani Road, P.O. Box 30715 Nairobi, Tel: 720760, £17.50/£23 ($33/$43.50).

Hotel Boulevard, Harry Thuku Road, P.O. Box 42831 Nairobi, Tel: 22756/9, £15/£18 ($28/$34).

Heron Court Apartment Hotel, Milimani Road, P.O. Box 41848 Nairobi, Tel: 720740/1/2/3, £6.50/£8.50 ($12.50/$16).

It is far less expensive, but still clean and safe, to spend the night in the hotels located east of Moi Avenue, (for example Iqbal Hotel) and in the area around Moktar Daddah Street (for example Terminal Hotel).

Automobile Association: →*Automobile Clubs*

Banks: Barclay's Bank, Kenyatta Avenue corner of Moi Avenue, open Monday to Saturday from 9 am to 4:30 pm. All of the larger hotels in the centre of the city have a currency exchange services.

Bars: The bars of the large hotels (with the exception of the Delamere Bar in the Norfolk Hotel) are nothing exceptional. Local clientele imbibe in "The Pub," in the "680 Hotel" or in the less refined drinking halls.

Car Rental: Among the numerous car rental agencies in Nairobi, some have gained a good reputation through their professionalism and reliability. These are:

AVIS, P.O. Box 49795. Offices at the airport (Tel: 822186), on Kenyatta Avenue (Tel: 336703/4) and in the Nairobi Hilton (Tel: 229576/229577).

Glory Car Hire, Tubman Road, P.O. Box 669669, Tel: 225024, 224428 or 222910. After 6 pm: 744531 or 746222.

Central Rent-a-Car, Fedha Towers, Standard Street, P.O. Box 42977, Tel: 222888.

Intasun, Kenwood House, Kimathi Street, P.O. Box 42977, Tel: 34061, 24037 or 334438.

Excursions: Most visitors leave Nairobi after a one-night stay to go on a safari through the national parks or travel down to the coast. Unfortunately, many sights worth a visit located in vicinity of the capital are never seen. Yet, Nairobi is a good place to start from on interesting one-day excursions.

→*Lake Naivasha* and →*Hell's Gate.*

Ngong Hills: At an altitude of 2,460 metres (8,091 feet), these are not hills but a rather lofty mountain chain southwest of Nairobi. In KiMaa, the Masai language, "ngong" means "knuckle." According to an old legend, they belong to a giant who, after his death, sank into the earth so deeply that only his knuckles protruded. A convincing image as can best be seen shortly before sunset from the observation platform at Kenyatta Conference Centre in Nairobi.

Located directly on the edge of the East African Rift, the Ngong Hills form a type of natural border between modern-day Kenya and pre-European Africa. On the hillsides facing Nairobi is a patchwork of small farms. On the other side, the Ngong Hills drop off into the rift forming breathtakingly steep steps. The arid savanna before the hills seems to have remained untouched for centuries, used by the Masai as pastureland for their herds for just as long. The Ngong Hills can be explored on foot as well as by car. Walking from observation point to observation point, one has — during good weather — a magnificent view of the skyline of Nairobi to the east and on the arid savanna to the west. With some luck, one may even have a view of Mount Kenya, the highest mountain in Kenya, beyond Nairobi. Unfortunately, some people walking through this park have made the unpleasant acquaintance of bandits. Those who drive to this park, should hire someone to accompany them at the police station in the little village of Ngong. The mountain ridge itself is accessible by car.

Olorgesaillie and Lake Magadi: Located 110 kilometres (68 miles) south of Nairobi, these prehistoric excavation sites are easily accessible by car via the excellent paved roadways. It is highly likely that one will stop more than once to enjoy the beautiful panoramas which line this road leading through the peaceful savanna. For this reason, it is advisable to start out very early in the morning to avoid a hectic pace. Lake Magadi is, at an altitude of 580 metres (1,903 feet), one of the lowest-lying lakes in the East African Rift. This makes it one of the hottest places in Kenya. It is absolutely necessary to bring along a large supply of beverages. Leaving Nairobi, the Langata Road, and later the Magadi Road, first ascends the southern slopes of the Ngong Hills. On the other side, the road winds down in a breathtaking serpentine into the rift. The lush vegetation gradually thins. After driving 65 kilometres (40 miles) one will reach Olorgesaillie. More than 40 years ago, the famous archeologist couple Louis and Mary Leakey excavated stone tools, round hammer stones and antelope bones from the Stone Age, as well as the remains of giant baboons and elephants. They made the discovery that this region was covered by a lake around 300,000 years ago, attracting animals and hunters alike. Human bones have yet to be found. From a small observation platform, one can recognise the basin of the prehistoric lake. Olorgesaillie was declared a national park in 1947, and a small museum was built. Straw-covered huts with showers and toilets offer lodging to visitors who plan to spend the night here. Camping is also possible.

Beyond Olorgesaillie, bizarre rock formations to both sides of Magadi Road dominate the scenery. The grade of the road becomes increasingly obvious, and the temperature rises noticeably. After driving almost one hour, Lake Magadi shimmers white on the horizon. It consists almost entirely of solid and semi-solid soda and its smell will be perceived by sensitive noses at quite a distance. At the lakeshore is the "Magadi Soda Company" workers' community, where the potash is quarried for export. The heat and the stench make this lake into an outpost of hell. One should drive on the dike leading across the lake in order to gain the full effect of this inconceivable landscape.

Medical Care: Medical care for tourists is of high standards in Nairobi. In addition to the medical emergency services offered by the international hotels, there are well equipped hospitals with excellent medical standards:

Nairobi Hospital, Argwings Kodhek Road, Tel: 722160/6.

The Aga Khan Hospital, 3rd Parklands Avenue, Tel: 742531.

Mater Misericordiae Hospital, South "B," Dunga Road, Tel: 556878.

Night Life: Since there are few cultural events in Nairobi, all nightly activities centre on the restaurants, cinemas and on dancing and drinking after sunset. The cinemas and discotheques in the centre of town are similar to those everywhere else. Pop music from the United States dominates; most of the clientele are white.

There is a total of 12 cinemas in Nairobi. Most of them show only cheap karate films and Indian love stories. Films of higher standards and even some prize-winning films are shown by:

20th Century, Mama Ngina Street, Tel: 2757.

Nairobi, Nkrumah Lane.

Kenya, Moi Avenue, Tel: 26981.

Clubs include:

New Florida Night Club, Koinange Street, Tel: 334870.

Visions, Kimathi Street, Tel: 332331. A favourite with teenagers.

Luke's Club, Kimathi Street, in 1990 *the* dance club in Nairobi.

Hollywood Night Club, Moktar Daddah Street, Tel: 27949.

Florida 2000, Moi Avenue. Dance club with shows.

Photographic Repair: A safari into the wilderness puts one's photographic equipment severely to the test. The dust and jolts can damage the equipment. All types of repaires are offered in the Camera Clinic (Biashara Street, Tel: 22492).

Restaurants: Since there are innumerable restaurants serving international cuisine in Nairobi, it can pose a problem finding a typically "African" meal. If the simple restaurants and snack bars in the east of the city are not to one's taste, one should try the restaurant at the *African Heritage* (Tel: 333157) on Kenyatta Avenue. In addition to traditional Kenyan food, they also have an Ethiopian buffet with a large array of dishes every Friday.

Ethiopian: Daas (in Grosvenor Hotel), Lenana Road, Tel: 727353 or 722080. Traditional Ethiopian cuisine.

Indian: Minar, Banda Street, open Monday to Saturday from 9:30 am to 2 pm and 5:30 to 10:15 pm, Sunday from 6:30 to 10 pm The Chicken Tika is especially tasty. Satkar, Moi Avenue, open daily from 7 to 9 pm South Indian vegetarian cuisine. Safeer, Tom Mboya Street (in the Ambassadeur Hotel), Tel: 336803, open Monday to Saturday from noon to 2:15 pm and 7 to 10:45 pm, Sunday from noon to 2 pm and 7 to 10 pm. Formal attire is required. The Reshni kebab (marinated chicken grilled over charcoal) is delicious.

Curry Pot, Moi Avenue, Tel: 28684. Hearty cuisine, always well frequented.
Dhaba, Keekorok Road, Tel: 222799, 334862. Excellent North Indian cuisine.
Chinese: Rickshaw, Fedha Towers, Tel: 223604. First-class restaurant where the high society meets.
Mandarin, Tom Mboya Street, open daily from noon to 2 pm and 7 to 10 pm, closed Sundays. One of, if not *the* most popular Chinese restaurant in Nairobi.
Hong Kong, Koinange Street, Tel: 228612. Cantonese cuisine.
China Garden, Aga Khan Walk.
Italian: Marino's, Aga Khan Walk, Tel: 336210/337230. Pizzas and pasta served by a friendly waiter.
Trattoria, Wabera Street corner of Kaunda Street, Tel: 340855. Pizzeria of higher standards with international clintele. Always well frequented.
La Cucina, Yaya Centre, Argwings Kodhek Road, Hurlingham, offering chaufeur service by contacting Tel: 56281/50.
French: Le Jardin de Paris, Loita Street corner of Monrovia Street (in the French cultural centre). Excellent soups and seafood.
Steak Houses: Maneaters Den, Moi Avenue, Tel: 331189. Serving all types of wild game.
Steak House Ltd., Chester House, Koinange Street, Tel: 23093. For the larger appetite: 1.2 kg T-bone-steak.
Angus, Aga Khan Walk. Excellent steaks and fillets, fresh salads.
Red Bull, Mama Ngina Street First class restaurant with a cozy atmosphere.
The Porterhouse (formerly Steak Palace), K.C.S. House, Mama Ngina Street, Tel: 224716, 221829.
Vegetarian: Happy Eater, Tubman Road, P.O. Box 42435 Nairobi, Tel: 220745. Vegetarian pizzas, salads, sandwiches etc. Nice, but nothing special.
The Norfolk Hotel, New Stanley Hotel as well as the hotel giants Hilton and Intercontinental have first-rate restaurants as welland are the best addresses for enjoying an extensive breakfast.

Safari Agencies →*Travel in Kenya*

Shopping: The commercial metropolis of Nairobi offers numerous areas with a large array of products and excellent shopping. Groceries and fresh fruits and vegetables are sold at the *City Market* on Muindi Mbingu Street. Beautiful batiks, colourful sisal shoulder bags and soapstone carvings are also available at the numerous sales stands along the streets. Sometimes pushy salespeople will try to force their merchandise on tourists, but one can browse through the selection at *African Heritage* on Kenyatta Avenue. The city's largest souvenir shop also has an excellent restaurant. The best address for buying everyday articles is *Biashara Street* in the eastern area of Nairobi, where all articles necessary for a successful safari in the wilderness (tents, paraffin lamps, folding spade, mess tins etc.) are available. *Colpro* (Kimathi Street), *Bella Boutique* (Kenyatta Avenue) and *Adelphi* (Kaunda Street) have specialised in selling light cotton clothing. The best book shops are the *Select Book Shop* (Kimathi Street), *Heritage* (Wabera Street) and the *Catholic Book Shop* (Mama Ngina Street), which not only offer imported literature but also a collection of African and Kenyan authors. Maps of the national parks are also available at these book shops.

Sports and Recreation: Those who plan on a longer stay in Nairobi, do not need to give up their favourite sports. Most of the sport clubs in and around Nairobi offer a temporary membership. It is better to call in advance to avoid unnecessary travelling.

Participation Sports: Impala Club, Ngong Road, P.O. Box 41516 Nairobi, Tel: 565684, 560638 or 766037. Tennis, squash, cricket, hockey, bridge. Nairobi Gymkhana, Rwathia/Forest Roads, P.O. Box 40116 Nairobi, Tel: 742938. Rugby, hockey, cricket.

Golf Courses: Karen Golf Club, Tel: 882801.

Muthaiga Golf Club, Tel: 767755/762400.

Royal Nairobi Golf Club, Tel: 725769/725768.

Mountaineering: Mountain Club of Kenya, P.O. Box 45741 Nairobi, Tel: 501747 (after 8:30 pm). The club members meet every Thursday at 8:30 pm in the club house at the Wilson Airport.

Chess: Nairobi Chess Club, P.O. Box 50443 Nairobi, Tel: 25007 (Mr. A. Adam). The members meet every Thursday at 5:30 pm in the French Cultural Centre, Loita Street corner of Monrovia Street.

Photography: Nairobi Photographic Society, P.O. Box 49879 Nairobi, Tel: 891075. The members meet every first and third Thursday at 5:30 pm at the Saint Johns Ambulance Headquarters.

Tourist Information: Tourist's Kenya, Union Towers, Moi Avenue, P.O. Box 40025 Nairobi, Tel: 337169/331274.

Information office of the Nairobi Publicity Association, Mama Ngina Street, P.O. Box 42278 Nairobi.

Transportation

Nairobi is not only one of the most important traffic hubs in Kenya, but it is also an international axis for trips into the neighbouring countries, to the islands in the Indian Ocean and to South Africa. During the night and in the early morning, planes from all over the world line the runway at the ultramodern Jomo Kenyatta Airport. Various charter flights take off from the Wilson Airport, taking passengers to all of the attractive destinations in East Africa. In addition, the main station of the Uganda Railways (now run by Kenya Railways) connects the capital with →*Mombasa* on the coast and →*Kisumu* on the banks of Lake Victoria. The Kenya railway is very popular among the tourists who want to travel around, because of the attentive personnel and the comfortable sleeper-cars. Last but not least, all important bus companies are also headquartered in Nairobi. Buses, long-distance taxis and the notorious matatus *(→Travel in Kenya)* bring their passengers from Nairobi to even the most remote corners of the country.

Air Travel: Kenya Airways flies at least six times daily to Mombasa, twice daily to Malindi, and four times daily to Kisumu. An economy class ticket costs around £16.50/$31. Information on departure times is available at the Kenya Airways office on Koinange Street (Tel. for reservations: 229291, 229271, 332750) or at the information counters in the airport (Tel: 822111).

Air France, Hilton Hotel, Mama Ngina Street, P.O. Box 30159 Nairobi, Tel: 728910/5.

Alitalia, Hilton Hotel, Mama Ngina Street, P.O.Box 72651 Nairobi, Tel: 24361/337439.

British Airways, International House, Mama Ngina Street, P.O. Box 45050 Nairobi, Tel: 334362/334440.

Egypt Air, Hilton Hotel, Mama Ngina Street, P.O. Box 44953 Nairobi, Tel: 26821/27683.

Iberia, Hilton Hotel, Mama Ngina Street, P.O. Box 60418 Nairobi, Tel: 338623/331648.

KLM, Fedha Towers, Muindi Mbingu Street, P.O. Box 49239 Nairobi, Tel: 332677.

Lufthansa, IPS Building, Kimathi Street, P.O. Box 30320 Nairobi, Tel: 335819/26271.

Sabena, International House, Mama Ngina Street, P.O. Box 43708 Nairobi, Tel: 22185/333284.

Swissair, Corner House, Kimathi Street, P.O. Box 44549 Nairobi, Tel: 331012/340231.

More than a dozen of small charter airlines are in a strong competition with the state-operated airline. They depart from the Wilson Airport and bring their passengers to all the points of interest in Kenya and the neighbouring countries including East Zaire.

The most reliable charter airlines are:

Pioneer Airlines, Wilson Airport, P.O. Box 43356 Nairobi, Tel: 501319/501399/500396.

Cooper Skybird Aircharters Ltd., c/o Bunson's Travel, Standard Street, Tel: 21992/2/4.

Skymmaster Ltd., Wilson Airport, P.O. Box 58771 Nairobi, Tel: 501608, 501593.

Train Travel: The fundamental difference between the trains of Kenya Railways and all other means of transportation in Kenya is that the trains are always on time! The night train to Mombasa, a 500 kilometre (312 miles) trip, is a tourist attraction in and of itself: departing at 5 pm (a second train departs from Nairobi at 7 pm), these pass through the Nairobi National Park shortly before sunset *(→Nairobi/Sights).*

Towards 7 pm, a waiter rings a bell to announce that dinner is served in the dining car. Those who are lucky enough will find a vacant seat in one of the old carriages from the colonial times. Most of the plates, knives and forks, and napkins still carry the trademark "Made in Great Britain." Bed linens and towels are available for a fee. In 1991, a special train for tourists was put into service, travelling the route through beautiful landscapes during daytime (among others through the *→Tsavo National Park).* Due to the British narrow-gauge rails, this trip takes almost 12 hours. Tourists prefer the first and the second class cars. For those who decide on this distinguished type of transportation, it is advisable to book the trip several days in advance directly at the train station (first class: £10/$18.75; second class: £4.75/$8.75).

Travel by Bus and Taxi: Most of the bus companies are located in the eastern part of the city. The Akamba Bus Service (Lagos Road) enjoys a very good reputation, since they service all parts of the country with buses in very good condition. These usually also arrive on time. Other, no less reliable companies are the Coastline Safari (Accra Road, services the coastal area), Goldline Coach Service (Accra Road, services the coastal region), East African Road Service (Racecourse Road, has busses to all parts of the country).

A little more expensive, but faster and more comfortable are the very popular long-distance taxis, usually Peugeot 504, Fiat or Nissan mini-buses. The most widely known companies are the Rift Valley Peugeot Service, RVP (Latema Road, West Kenya, Mombasa Peugeot Service (Duruma Road, coast) and Malindi Taxi Ltd. (Accra Road, coast).

Nudism

Swimming or sunbathing nude is absolutely prohibited. On the grounds of the beach hotels, bathing topless is permitted.

Nyeri

(population: 5,000; altitude: 1,950 metres/6,398 feet)

Nyeri is the inofficial capital of the Kikuyu people, located 115 kilometres (72 miles) north of Nairobi in a broad valley between Mount Kenya and the foothills of the Aberdare Mountains. In earlier times, the town was a centre of the British coffee

planters who soon discovered that this area was high in agricultural value and set up large plantations. They were the first to be affected by the Mau-Mau upheavals in the 50's, since the guerrillas operated from their bases in the impenetrable woods of the Aberdares. Meanwhile, most of the white farmers have left Kenya. The streets of Nyeri are still lively despite this. From early morning to sunset, the products of this region are sold on the market, in the shops and in the "dukas": tea, coffee, potatoes, tomatoes, millet, beans, nuts, sugar-cane, cassada, pumpkins, mango and passion fruit as well as cooking bananas. Walking through this lively town, it is almost palpable that this region has one of the highest population densities. Every square mile is used in agriculture. For those interested: the Sir Robert Stevenson Baden-Powell memorial is located at the Outspan Hotel. He was the founder of the scouts and died in Nyeri in 1941.
Most of the tourists only know Nyeri as a in-between stop on their way to the →*Aberdare National Park.* Those who would like to spend a night in the Treetops Hotel (which has already gained a legendary reputation) have their last chance to make a reservation in the Outspan in Nyeri; there is no other way to reserve a room. A stay at this hotel is certainly quite expensive, but one can be certain to sleep in the most luxurious and traditional hotel ever to be built in the African bush. Royalty and famous statesmen have stayed in this hotel, for example, Queen Elizabeth learned of her father's death and her ascent to the English throne in the Treetops Hotel. Three years later, the Treetops was totally completely destroyed in a Mau-Mau guerrilla attack. The hotel which replaced it was built on stilts and is even larger, but has no less atmosphere. An observation platform provides a view of the waterhole and saltlick below which attract various kinds of big game, including elephants and leopards. However, the big show takes place after sunset, when the vivid scenery is illuminated by floodlights, and most of the park's animals can be observed when they gather at the waterhole.

Nyeri / **Practical Information**

Accomodation

Outspan Hotel, P.O. Box 23 Nyeri, Tel: 2424, £32.50/£40.25 ($61/$75.50). This beautiful hotel was built in 1927 in the British colonial style, and is located in the centre of a groomed park. Mount Kenya can be seen from the rooms in the northern wing of the building. The management organises not only a night in the Treetops, but also interesting sight-seeing tours to the local coffee and tea plantations.

Treetops, c/o P.O. Box 23 Nyeri or c/o P.O. Box 47557 Nairobi, Tel: 335807, £36.50/£53 ($68.50/$100).
White Rhino Hotel, Nairobi Road, P.O. Box 30 Nyeri, Tel: 2189, 2013.

Public Transportation →*Travel in Kenya*
Olorgesaillie →*Nairobi/Practical Information, Excursions*

The People of Kenya

97% of the total population of Kenya are Africans, belonging to 42 different ethnic groups. There are three linguistic families represented in Kenya: the Bantu languages, the Nilotic languages and the Cushitic languages. The largest groups among the Bantu languages are the Kikuyu (3.6 million), the Luhya (2.3 million) and the Kamba (1.9 million). When including the other Bantu language groups, these make up two thirds of the total population. The leading group in terms of numbers speaking Nilotic languages are the Luo (2.2 million), followed by the Kalenjin (including the Kipsigis, Marakwet, Tugen; 1.7 million) and the Masai (250,000). The Cushitans (all Galla and Somali ethnic groups) represent only 3% of the total population.
Originally, the lines were clearly drawn: the Bantu people tended fields, the Nilotes were nomads and raised cattle. Through the centuries of contact between these groups, however, more and more nomads took up farming. The Luo and the Kalenjin in the Lake Victoria region have been farmers and fishermen for generations. Forced by the external conditions, the Turkana and some subordinate clans of the Masai have only recently given up their nomadic lifestyle.
Today, approximately 23 million people live in Kenya. Of these 65,000 are Europeans (about 7,000 with Kenyan citizenship), 200,000 Asians (Indians and Pakistani, some of which hold a British passport) as well as 42,000 Arab nationals. The growth rate of the population is 4% and is one of the highest in the world. Governmental campaigns promoting contraception in order to prevent a population explosion have had only limited success. The average life expectancy in Kenya is 56 years of age. Kenya's most difficult problems are the exodus to rural regions from the overpopulated areas of north of Nairobi and the Lake Victoria region, which have a population density of 500 per square kilometre (1,280 per square mile) as well as wide-spread unemployment in the cities. This is compounded by tribal cliques (tribalism, which is prevalent throughout Africa) form interest groups in politics and the economy make for an atmosphere of conflict rather than cooperation.

Pharmacies

In every larger city in Kenya, there is at least one well-stocked pharmacy (also called ''chemistry'' or ''duka ya dawa''). In general, these are open until 9 pm. A list of the pharmacies with emergency service can be found in the daily newspaper. Nevertheless, it is easier to bring along an adequate supply of any prescription medications taken regularly.

→*Medication*

Photography

Kenya is an El Dorado for avid photographers. Since there is an enormous variety of motifs worth photographing, it is advisable to bring along a camera with additional lenses (among others a 200mm lens for close-ups in the national parks). Lenscaps and daylight filters are absolutely imperative to protect the sensitive lens against the dust. Additional batteries should also be brought along, as well as a large supply of film since these are very expensive in Kenya and often stocked too long. After 20 years of tourism, many Kenyans have began to react surly, or even aggressively, whenever a camera is focussed on them. Thus, it is better to ask for permission in advance, and chat a little bit, or to offer some money or something to barter. It is prohibited to take pictures of the national flag and of the president, as well as military facilities, prisons and their inmates, and the old port of Mombasa (this is because inmates work there). Also be careful when taking pictures of train stations, bridges, industrial facilities and other installations of strategic interest.

Police

Contact between tourists and the Kenyan police is limited. This is not due to extremely considerate behaviour on the part of guests to the country, but because of the high level of restraint practised by the native police officers. This is especially true for traffic regulation: rental cars with tourists seated in them are generally waved through at roadblocks. However, this does not mean that one is able to drive as one pleases. If one is caught in a radar trap (especially in and around Nairobi and along the coast), polite conduct is highly advisable and one should be as cooperative as possible. Otherwise, it is very possible that the police officers will take advantage of the rare opportunity to mercilessly draw out the privileged person's suspense for quite as while... and demand money. If one does get lost on a tour through Kenya, if the car breaks down or if a place to stay the night cannot be found, then the Kenyan police will do everything in their power to help tourists out of a pinch.

If, however, one is caught in possession of drugs or in black market activities, then the friendly, helpful conduct of the police understandable grinds to a halt. In the most extreme cases, one must count on a prison sentence or deportation.

Politics

During the first 15 years of independence beginning in 1963, Kenya gained the reputation of being the "Switzerland of Africa" thanks to the stability of its domestic politics. This was the product of the unifying personality of the first President Jomo Kenyatta *(→History)*. He succeeded in conveying a new — a Kenyan — national identity to the 40 ethnic groups living within the young nation with his slogan "Harambee" (which means as much as to pull together on the same rope). Politics and economy have been gradually Africanised, and the British settlers who have not yet left the country were compensated generously. This continuing process did not progress without friction. The native class of bureaucrats from the colonial period became the new ruling class after Kenya attained its independence. They nurtured personal advantage, and gained immense wealth. They transformed domestic policy into a confusing jumble of interest groups pitted against each other clinging only to their tribal mindset. Thus, the Kikuyu tribe dominated under the leadership of Kenyatta, one of their own tribal members. The key positions in politics, the military and administration were filled by people from this ethnic group, while members of the Lou and other ethnic groups were given only insignificant positions. After the death of the "Mzee" on August 22, 1978, Daniel arap Moi succeeded him in office. Fortunately, the expected uprisings did not occur. Moi himself was a Tugen from the Kalenjin *(→People)* pursued a policy of levelling out friction between the tribal groups during the first ten years. He introduced the slogan "Nyayo" (loosely translated: in the footsteps of the old man). He forced the Kikuyus out of their dominant role in the administration, resorting to means on the border of legality. Further political initiatives of the early years were combating corruption, smuggling and the black market as well as reducing the overgenerous distribution of land to supporters of the governmental party. However, Moi stomached political opposition even worse than his predecessor. Faced with the rapidly deteriorating economic situation, sectors of the military and the students in Nairobi attempted a coup d'état. Moi reacted violently. Hundreds of people lost their lives in the clash, which lasted seven days. Following these events, he publicly proclaimed the one-party state (which de facto already existed) and the absolute power of the KANU party. The government does not lack initiatives to solve its existential problems — the increasing cleft between the rich and the poor, extreme unemployment and the population explosion. When confronted with these dilemmas, the initiatives could hardly have an effect on the situation. Since the idea of Perestroika has also lapped over into Africa, many governments have given in to their people's demand for pluralism and free elections. Even so, Kenya's dictator Moi is still one of the hardliners to date. He silenced critics of the state by arguing that ''only one bull can be in a pen.'' The opposition was treated quite ruthlessly. The assassination of the Minister of Foreign Affairs Robert Ouko at the beginning of 1990 and the subsequent investigations, the findings which resulted have been kept under lock and key by Moi — probably for good reason. In July 1990, twenty oppositional demonstrators were shot to death by the police in Nairobi and other cities. The mysterious, accidental death of Muge, the popular archbishop and critic of the government, as well as published incidents of torture of imprisoned opponents brought Amnesty International to the country. In 1991, the international press confirmed that the Kenyan administration was getting increasingly nervous. Moi reacted to the domestic unrest with a dangerous balancing act of promised reforms and reprisals. It was only at the end of 1991, that he publicly accepted the establishment of new political parties and agreed to free elections. How these developments are to be evaluated, remains to be seen.

Postal System

There is a post office in every larger village (business hours: Monday to Friday from 8 am to 1 pm and 2 to 4:30 or 5 pm). The General Post Offices in Nairobi (Kenyatta Avenue and Haile Selassie Avenue) and in Mombasa (Digo Road) are also open on Saturday morning as well as on Sunday from 9 am to 10 am. An air-mail letter to Europe costs 6.50 KSH; postcards and aerograms, 4.50 KSH. In general, it takes four to eight days to reach their destination.

Religion

Kenya is a multicultural state with numerous religions and religious beliefs, coexisting more or less peacefully. Along the coast as well as in the northeast of the country, the Islam is obviously the dominating religion whose followers are Sunnite Moslems. The Ismaelitic congregation is well represented in Kenya. Though fundamental Shi'its have not yet settled into society, the growing economic and social problems have recently resulted in intolerance and tensions between the Moslems and the Christians. Hinduism came to the country before the first Europeans set foot in Kenya. Hinduism grew in importance through the Indian contract workers, brought to the country when the Uganda railway was built. Hindu and Sikh temples are scattered all over the country, especially prevalent in places with a railway station.

In the middle of the 19th century, Christian missionaries came to the country. They belonged to different denominations and were in merciless competition fighting it out for African souls. By forcing the "poor heathens" to become above all good Catholics, Protestants, Anglicans, Baptists and Lutherans, they caused the religious segmentation still apparent today. However, an increasing number of Kenyans do not feel uncomfortable as members of the missionary churches and join the independent separatists' churches or sects founded by native Africans. Traditional elements like dancing and singing, healing and revelation through dreams and visions play an important role in these services.

Although 30% of the total population professes the Islamic failth and 60% the Christian faith, traditional religious beliefs have not been abandoned. During the pre-European times the concept of a supreme being already existed, which helped the missionaries to their success. The spirits of the ancestors are still consulted for advice on important occasions, and in the rural areas, the ill still consult a traditional medicine man before going to a hospital.

Restaurants

One can be sure not to starve in Kenya. However, those who travel in the country on their own cannot expect *haut cuisine* — in Kenya, the government is always relieved to have been able to feed the populace for another year. From this follows that the mediocre "hoteli" do not offer food that could please a gourmet palate, but mostly chicken, fish or grilled goat meat, and as a side dish rice, beans or chips. In general, the food is well digestible, though the plates, forks and knives seem to have just been washed in very old dishwater — ketchup from the plastic squeeze bottles helps to overcome any lingering doubts. This is as much a part of the standard furnishings as the greasy, clogged salt-shaker and the skinny cat rubbing against one's legs. Making a stop at a "hoteli" (no accommodation is offered) is fun, not lastly because of the colourful waiter regards a "wazungu" — (Swahili for "white") guest as a welcome diversion. Tea is served with a lot of milk and sweetened with so much sugar that even the first drop is an all out attack on one's teeth. Bottled beer and soft drinks are available almost everywhere, but these are not always served chilled.

On the other side of the spectrum are the restaurants with European standards. Those who are in Kenya for the first time, usually expected anything but such a wide variety of excellent restaurants serving specialties from all over the world and gourmet cuisine. Italian, Chinese, Spanish, Indian, French and German food, and of course, the international junk food-culture. There is no problem finding these, at least not in Nairobi and Mombasa or in most of the larger cities. One almost feels at home: traditional African dishes are missing from the menu, making it easy to forget that one is in Africa.

Saiwa Swamp National Park

Covering only 2 square kilometres (0.75 square miles), it is the smallest national park in Kenya, located about 20 kilometres (12½ miles) north of the district capital →*Kitale.* This park is especially attractive since, in contrast to all other reserves, it must be explored on foot. Thanks to the absence of big game it is absolutely safe to walk through the park, consisting of picturesque gallery forests. The main attraction is the shy Sitatunga antelope which can only be observed so well in this swamp area. A number of narrow pathways lead through the evergreen forest, with long-tailed monkeys, Colobus apes as well as numerous kinds of birds roosted in the branches. Take a whole day to thoroughly enjoy this piece of untouched nature — and even spend a night in this park. Self-catering campsites are located in idyllic landscapes.

For more information, contact P.O. Box 753 Kitale, Tel: 22.

→*Kitale*

Samburu-Buffalo Springs Game Reserve

This game reserve is very different from those south of the equator with lush vegetation and a large stock of game. This reserve was set up at the beginning of the 1970's and is located 314 kilometres (196 miles) from Nairobi in the former Northern Frontier District *(→Lake Turkana).* Lowlands glimmer in the heat north of Mount Kenya. Dry buffalo grass, thorn bushes, and from time to time acacia groves dominate this area covering 337 square kilometres (131 square miles). Early in the morning and shortly before dusk, one has a clear view of the snow-capped summit of Mount Kenya with its green hills and the picturesque forests interspersed with elegant dum palms along the Ewaso Nyiro River make for an attractive contrast. Since this reservoir in the savanna never dries up, many kinds of animals are attracted here. In addition to buffaloes, a large herd of elephants, lions, leopards and cheetahs, the smallest kind of antelope existing, the delicate rabbit-sized dikdik also lives in this area. This reserve has become famous for its three rare species, the only of their kind living north of the equator. The long-necked gerenuk, also called Waller's gazelle, is the only kind of antelope which rears up to its hind legs in order to reach the green leaves on the higher branches. The Grevy zebra is bigger than its cousin in the south, and can be recognised by its thin stripes and thick mane. In the northern part of the reserve, one often sees the so called Somali ostrich which can be recognised by its rather bluish legs different from the pink legs typical for ostriches.

A special attraction are the Buffalo Springs in the east of the reserve. Run-off from Mount Kenya bubbles back up to the surface in a number of clear spring basins. The largest of these was fortified during the Second World War in order to be used by British soldiers on their way up to Abyssinia as a welcome bathing facility. Now individual sweat-stained travellers also dive into the ponds. However, caution is advised: according to unconfirmed reports, apart from harmless animals, a crocodile may also lurk into the pool. However, the water is so clear that a glimpse into the pool is enough to confirm that one can swim without any unpleasant company.

Samburu-Buffalo Springs Reserve / **Practical information**

Accomodation

Buffalo Springs Lodge, P.O. Box 71 Isiolo or P.O. Box 30471
Nairobi, Tel: 336858, £29/£37 ($55/$70). Luxury campsite with tents in the swamp areas, where many animals live, generous price reduction during off-season.
Samburu Serena Lodge, P.O. Box 48690 Nairobi, Tel: 339800,
£36.50/£48 ($68.50/$91). Also offers reduced prices during the low season.
Along the so-called Champagne Ridge, shortly after the Ngare Mara Gate, there are some self-catering campsites.

Shimba Hills National Reserve

This wildlife reserve in Shimba Hills is one of the protected areas in Kenya which is the least frequented by tourists — although it is only a short distance away from the beach hotels of Mombasa. This might be due to the fact that the animals can only be seen with difficulty among the thick underbrush than is the case in the broad savannas of the →*Tsavo National Park*. This means there is no guarantee that visitors will be able to focus their cameras on the largest number of animals in the shortest possible period of time.

This should, however, not be the goal of a safari in any case. One should sooner rent a car for a trip to the Shimba Hills and devote an entire day to discovering the park, exploring the area of 192 square kilometres (74 square miles) at a relaxed pace. In contrast to the heat and humidity on the coast, the cool jungle air is pleasantly refreshing at this altitude of 500 metres (1,640 feet). Adventurous paths lead to observation points and picnic places, where one can even see the ocean and all the way to Mombasa, given clear weather.
This reserve was founded to protect the horse-sized sabre antelope which only live in this region of Kenya. These can be easily recognised by their impressive antlers in the form of sabres. They can most commonly be spotted in the area between the Lango-Magandi Forest and the Giriama Hill observation point. The herd of elephants is constantly on the move making it impossible to say where they might be at a given time. It is best to inquire at the entrance to the park where the herd has been most recently spotted. When hiking through the region, fresh elephant dung on the pathways may be of help in tracking them. There are only a few large breeds of cats, African buffaloes, giraffes and some baboon troops.

Shimba Hills / **Practical Information**

Accommodation

Shimba Lodge, reservations can be made by contacting: Nyali Beach Hotel, Tel: 471551 or 471567/8 in Mombasa. Prices are £30 ($55) per person. This is a brand new, luxurious tree house directly at a water hole. Guided hiking tours through the wildlife reserve are also offered.
Three km (2 miles) from the main entrance is a camping area equipped with showers and toilets. This is situated on a rugged cliff.

Shopping

The business hours in the big cities in Kenya are from 8 am to 5:30 or 6:30 pm. The shops located in the country are also popular, often places where young villagers meet, and are open until late in the night.
There are souvenirs to suit every taste in Kenya. Special articles include artistic soapstone carvings, sold all over the country, and beautiful sisal bags (''kyondo,'' pl. ''vyondo''), produced mainly by Kikuyu women at home. Meanwhile, traditional articles such as Masai and Turkana headrests, shields, amulets and jewellry are also produced for the tourists.
The colourful cotton scarves (''kanga'') printed with partly traditional, partly modern motifs, have a number of uses. The hem is decorated with morals or sometimes

even humorous epigrams in Swahili. The equivalent for men is the ''kikoi'' (pl. vikoi), a solid and rather plain scarf worn by men along the coast. Kenyan coffee and tea, coffee liqueur (''Kenya Gold'') and the papaya wine which has been successfully produced in Kenya for several years, have also become increasingly popular as souvenirs.

Sights

Kenya has a little of everything — a country of inconceivable diversity. In this country with an area the size of the Iberian peninsula are tropical sandy beaches as well as mountain peaks blanketed in perennial ice, hostile deserts and fertile grasslands.
Even the first Europeans to arrive in this country were aware of the touristic potential of Kenya. Officers and settlers enjoyed spending their holidays on the coast, while wealthy noblemen and businessmen went on big game hunts and British retirees settled in the highlands after brining their professional life to a close because of the healthy climate. It is for this reason that many a hotel was built during this period as for example, the Norfolk in Nairobi and the Treetops Hotel near Nyeri. Mass tourism began at the end of the 1960's. From this time on, Kenya — along with Thailand, Sri Lanka and Cuba — established itself as a holiday destination. Beautiful natural spectacles and above all the magnificent diversity of wildlife make this young country a microcosm of the African continent: wild animals, exotic peoples, vast untouched landscapes and deserted beaches that one can only dream of. The combination of a beach holiday and safari tourism has become the classic form for a holiday in Kenya. Meanwhile, there are more than forty big game and nature reserves. The most significant of these are described in detail in this guide. The Kenyan government continued the protective policies of the colonial administration, which had already established the first reserve in East Africa in 1900: the Nairobi National Park *(→Nairobi / Sights).* However, these reserves were not founded for the tourists, as evidenced by their classifications. Within ''national parks,'' the entire natural conditions are under protection including animals, plant life and landscapes; in the ''game reserves'' and ''national reserves,'' only the animals stand under protection. The land may be used agriculturally by the population, as is the case with the Masai Mara Game Reserve, for example.
Nairobi is the centre for safari tourism, serving as a base and point of departure for excursions. Those who spend their holidays on the coast will set their sights on *Tsavo National Park,* located nearest to the coastal region; however, it is also possible to reach every safari destination in Kenya in the shortest amount of time

by charter plane. In general, the parks and nature reserves are open throughout the year. During the rainy season, however, road conditions are not as good as during the remainder of the year *(→Climate, Tourist Season).* This is especially true for national parks and nature reserves located in the highlands: *→Aberdare National Park* and *→Meru National Park* are temporarily inaccessible during this time.

Sibiloi National Park *→Lake Turkana-East Side / Sights*

Speed Limits

Yes, they do exist... but actually nobody in Kenya pays much attention to them. Everyone drives as fast as the road conditions or the car allows, meaning that one is confronted with absolutely fearless drivers as well as sluggish automobiles driven at a snail's pace. One must adapt driving to the situation on the roads. For example, one must always be aware of the deep potholes — even in the centre of Nairobi and Mombasa — of cattle herds on roads covered with dung as well as of chaotic pedestrians and cyclists. By the way, the speed limit in the city is 50 kilometres (about 31 miles) per hour, while on the country roads it is 100 kilometres (about 62 miles) per hour. Rental cars are not allowed to be driven faster than 65 kilometres (about 40 miles) per hour. Meanwhile, there are frequent radar controls on the arterial roads and on the roads along the coast.

Sports and Recreation

Even after having travelled thousands of miles from home, one still need not forgo one's favourite sports and recreational activities. In Nairobi, there are a number of sports clubs available *(→Nairobi / Practical Information).* Of course, water sports dominate the palette of free time activities along the coast. The appropriate equipment can be rented in the hotels: from diving gear and surfboards to outboard motorboats. The selection is supplemented by tennis courts, soccer fields and even squash courts and saunas. Some of the hotels also have rental bicycles *(→Beaches).* Usually, the sports equipment is in good condition. If this is not the case, then a replacement will be provided immediately.

Telephone

Communication by telephone is generally good in Kenya. There is a direct dial system between the cities. Especially in the rural areas the telephones date back to the colonial time and have to be cranked by hand. One needs 50 cent and 1 shilling coins for calls from the public telephones.

Internationals calls better are made at a hotel or at a General Post Office. Rates drop 40% between 10 pm and 10 am. Meanwhile, telephone cards (card phones) have become popular in Kenya. These are available at the General Post Offices in →*Nairobi, Mombasa, Nakuru* and *Kisumu.*
Emergency number: 999
Operator: 900

Theft

Statistics of recent years show a dramatic increase in crimes involving tourists and their property — showing that the economic and social condition of the majority of the people is getting worse heading toward a crisis. In Kenya, the differences in income are enormous. It is not surprising that many, especially young Kenyans confronted with the tourists' lifestyle choose the direct way of ''earning'' money. The government counters this development with draconic punishments, but without any real success.

Still in operation: ''African Queen'' steamboats connect the towns along the shores of Lake Victoria

Valuables and documents are best deposited in the safe at the tourist hotels (the inexpensive lodges of the inland areas also have safe deposit facilities). It is always advisable to leave one's valuables at a safe place in the hotel, whether one spends a day at the beach, strolls through the town or goes on a safari. An inconspicuous bag is sufficient for one's photographic equipment, traveller's cheques are well protected in a money belt, but leaving some banknotes peaking out of ones back pockets, and coins in the front pockets. As a rule of thumb: the less one carries along, the less one runs the risk of being robbed *(→Equipment).* In general, it is just as true for Kenya as for other countries: it is more dangerous to stay in the cities and in the tourist centres than in the country and in the wilderness. It is always advisable to be attentive and to be on the watch when in confusing situations (in buses, queues, at night in Nairobi and Mombasa). Meanwhile, the residents have gotten into the habit of persuing thieves who have been caught red-handed and have, unfortunately, started to lynch the culprit on more than one occasion. This should be kept in mind before one shouts for help. It is better to report the case to the police, though Kenyan law enforcement is sluggish *(→Police).*

The largest baobab in the country can be found in Ukunda at the experimental farm

Time of Day

Kenya is two hours later than Central Euopean time (during summer one hour later), three hours later than in the United Kingdom and 8 (New York) to 11 (Los Angeles) hours later than the United States. The sun rises around 6 am; around 6 pm it gets dark within 15 minutes.

Tipping

Service is usually included in the bills at tourist restaurants and hotels. Nevertheless, since the service personnel are usually very friendly and attentive, but earn very low wages, it is certainly a good idea to show one's gratitude by leaving a tip. How much — this is left to one's own descretion — the customary rate is 10%.

Tourist Information

Great Britain:

Kenya Tourist Office, 25 Brooks May off Davis Street, Mayfair, London OEY ELG, Tel: 071 355 314.

United States:

Kenya Tourist Office, New York, Downtown, 424 Madison Avenue, N.Y. 10017, U.S.A. The relevant travel literature on Kenya is a good source of information when planning a trip through Kenya *(→Literature).*

Tourist Season

Tourism specialists have divided the year in Kenya as follows:

The main season is from December 1 to March 31, and from June 1 to August 31. Low is during the rains in April and May as well as in September, October and November. In contrast to the heavy rains typical for equatorial Africa, on the Kenyan coast and in the highlands it rains only at night. During the daytime, short periods of rain are followed by sunshine. It is especially attractive to travel during this time not only because is much less expensive but also because this is when the vegetation is in full bloom.

Traffic

Driving on Kenyan streets is only half as dangerous and adventuresome as is often assumed. One can run into dangerous borderline situations everywhere, and common sense is always better than heroism and foolishness. However, it is advisable to be careful when one is confronted by a bus or one of the notorious matatus on the roads *(→Travel in Kenya).* Reduce the speed and keep as far to the left

(a relict from the British colonial period) as possible. The speed limits in the city is 50 kilometres (about 31 miles) per hour, on the country roads 100 kilometres (about 62 miles) per hour. Rental cars are not allowed to be driven faster than 65 kilometres (about 40 miles) per hour — nobody knows why, and nobody obeys this rule. Only recently put into force: safety belts are mandatory.
→*Automobile Clubs, Travel in Kenya*

Train Travel →*Travel in Kenya*

Travel Documents

Upon entry, one needs only a passport which must be valid for at least the next 6 months. Children must be registered in the passport of one of its parents or have a children's passport. The Kenyan stamp in the passport is considered a tourist visa, valid for three months. Those who want to stay longer than three months can apply for an extention at the Immigration Officece at Nyayo House, Posta Road, Nairobi (right behind the former General Post Office on Kenyatta Avenue). In general, an extention of one to two months is possible. A violation of the right of residency may have unpleasant consequences, or may even result in being arrested for several days.

Though no longer required, the following can prove useful:
an international vaccination card *(→Vaccinations),* if medical treatment is needed, the international driving licence in case of traffic controls, the youth hostel card to avoid additional fees for admission to the Kenyan Youth Hostel Association, and, as the case may be, the international student identification card, since there are sometimes discounted admission fees for students.

Travel in Kenya

In contrast to the other African states, Kenya was a colony (similar to Zimbabwe, formerly Rhodesia) right from the start. White settlers established a complete infrastructure according to their needs, which did not reflect the needs of the natives. This is the reason that Kenya has an extensive network of roadways and rails. Today, Kenya has more than 50,000 km (31,250 miles) of roadways, about 5,000 km (3,125 miles) of which are paved. although the quality of the Kenyan road system is far beyond the pitiful Central or West African road conditions, even the modern motorways (for example Nairobi — Mombasa) may have unpleasant surprises in store. The soft shoulders of the roads having been washed away, potholes like bomb craters and smeary cattle dung, especially around Mount Kenya, turn driv-

ing in Kenya into an adventuresome experience. Those who are on the road with a rental car, should plan on arriving at their destination before nightfall. It becomes dark quickly and unexpectedly early (i.e. around 6 pm) for those who are in Kenya for the first time. Apart from these obstacles, it is also difficult to recognise Kenyan pedestrians and cyclists on streets with insufficient lighting. Depending on circumstances, driving at night may become aggrivating — and dangerous.
In short: with the help of some improvisation, one will reach every destination in Kenya. Also, numerous bus and taxi companies, rental car agencies and safari organisations, railways going across the country, the state Carrier Kenya Airways as well as more than a dozen private charter airlines ensure a functioning transportation network in Kenya.

Travel in Kenya / **Buses, Taxis, Matatus**

These are the backbone of the Kenyan transportation system. There is probably no place in the country which is not served by these inexpensive means of transport. Those who want to go by bus or long-distance taxi should make a reservation at least one day in advance, especially for trips on the main artery connecting Nairobi and Mombasa and for destinations in the highly populated highlands. Most of the companies are located in Nairobi *(→Nairobi/Practical Information).* The ticket offices in the other towns and villages can be easily found: they are a part of the bus stations. Even new-comers to Kenya will find these bus stations quickly since they can either not be overlooked in small villages of a few hundred inhabitants, or cannot be overheard, for these are the centre of the organised chaos. Some information about the matatus: these are private vehicles, mostly a Peugeot or Nissan, which have been converted to accommodate passengers. They are much less expensive than buses and taxis and are preferred by the native residents. Because of the severe competition between the owners of the matatus and the bus companies the matatus are always overcrowded, packed with up to 30 passengers (motto: everyone *will* get in!) and they operate around the clock. Since these rickety vehicles mostly do not have the technical equipment necessary to bear the increased weight, more than 80% of them are virtual deathtraps. The newspapers report daily on matatus crashes with an average of 10 people having been killed. It is advisable to think twice whether your interest in local colour and customs is worth the risk...

→Rental Cars, Nairobi/Practical Information (addresses)

Travel in Kenya / **Safari Agencies**

''Safari'' is Kiswahili for ''travel,'' and there are a number of options to go on a safari as well as on excursions, day trips and expeditions — within Kenya as well as beyond its borders. It is surprising how easily the word ''safari'' becomes part of one's vocabulary.

Most of the country's attractions are located far away from the capital. Buses and matatus must stop at the entrances to the national parks. There are two possibilities to reach these places: Either by renting a car in Nairobi *(→Nairobi/Practical Information)* or Mombasa *(→Mombasa/Practical information)* and organising the tour oneself, or by contacting a safari agency. The range of tours offered consists of half-day sightseeing tours in Nairobi as well as standard 3 to 5 day trips through *→Amboseli* and *→Tsavo National Park* and even of expeditions to Tanzania, Ruanda and East-Zaire lasting several weeks.

Tours are offered to suit every taste; a difference is made between luxury safaris, offering their clients every comfort imaginable in the wilderness, and the camping

The legendary Turkana bus transports daring tourists into Kenya's hostile northern regions of Kenya

safaris, on which trucks jolt their passengers through Kenya. Nevertheless, the camping safaris are a booming enterprise since the experience of a dusty trip together with a colourful group of people and of the African nights when sitting around a campfire is much more intense than sitting in a luxury lodge in the centre of a savanna and sipping on a ''sundowner.''

Prices for orientation: a four-day safari through the Masai Mara National Reserve costs about £100/$187.50, a tour through Amboseli and Tsava about £100 to £116,50/$187.50 to $218.50 (sleeping in tents, three meals, admission fee included). The luxury tours of this type cost about twice as much.

Most of the following agencies in Nairobi offer both types of safaris. The following have a good reputation:

Gametrackers, Finance House, corner of Banda Street/Loita Street, P.O. Box 62041 Nairobi, Tel: 338927/22703. Also offering bicycle tours lasting several days.

Safari Seekers, Jubilee Insurance Exchange Building, Kaunda Street Nairobi, Tel: 26206/3345585.

Special Camping Safaris, Gilfillan House, Kenyatta Avenue, P.0. Box 51512 Nairobi, Tel: 338325. Reputable organizor of the legendary Lake Turkana Safaris.

Scenic Safaris Ltd., Westminster House, Kenyatta Avenue, P.O. Box 49188 Nairobi, Tel: 26526/29092. Offer relatively inexpensiv luxury safaris.

Yare Safaris Co. Ltd., Union Towers, Moi Avenue corner of Mama Ngina Street, P.O. Box 63006 Nairobi, Tel: 725610. Tours to Tansania, Zimbabwe and Ruanda.

Savage Wilderness Safaris, P.O. Box 44827 Nairobi, Tel: 521590. Canoe tours on the Galana River.

Bateleur Safaris, P.O. Box 42562 Nairobi, Tel: 27048. Specialised in bird-watching and hiking tours.

Travel in Kenya / **Trains**

Kenya Railways offer to tourists who like to travel much around an attractive alternative to buses and long-distance taxis. Very popular among travellers is the route Nairobi — Mombasa. Excellent 1st and 2nd class sleeping cars *(→Nairobi/Practical Information)* are available. Shortly before sunset the train passes through the Nairobi National Park *(→Nairobi/Sights),* allowing the passengers to see a number of animals. One has dinner and breakfast in the dining car. Clean bed linens for the night are available for a small fee.

The route Nairobi — Kisumu also leads through a beautiful landscape. Shortly after having left the capital, the train descends the steep walls of the East African Rift on the adventursome rails. The railways has no longer served the cities *→Kitale, Thika* and Nyahururu for several years.

Travelling to Kenya

In the age of long-distance tourism, most visitors come to Kenya by air. The Jomo-Kenyatta Airport in Nairobi serves more than 40 airlines from all over the world. The Moi Airport in Mombasa is, for the most part, for charter airlines and package tourists.

In autumn 1991, a plane ticket from Europe to Kenya cost between £420 and £534 ($782 and $1,000) depending on how long the visitor wanted to stay in the country. The following airlines have less expensive fares: Egypt Air, Aeroflot (however, with a stopover in Moskow), Iberia and Olympic Airways. Those who plan on staying two or three weeks, should consider booking a package tour. During the low season (→*Tourist Season),* a three-week-stay can cost as little as £670 ($1,250).

Tsavo National Park

Covering 20,720 square kilometres (8,000 square miles), the Tsavo National Park is larger than all other parks in Kenya together. For administrative reasons, the park was divided into Tsavo East and Tsavo West. The Mombasa Highway and the Railways cross the park right through the centre. Nevertheless, one does not get lost within the extensive wilderness of the park which is not only the habitat of 60 kinds of mammals and 500 kinds of birds, but also offers about of 1,250 miles (2,000 kilometres) of roadways passable for normal cars, as well as excellent accommodations. The Tsavo East is only partly open for the public. The region north of the Galana River was declared off limits.

Among tourists, the Tsavo West is preferred to the other side of the park, since it has a more varied landscape. The Tsavo River divides it into two halves. South of the river, the bushland increasingly gives way to the open savanna. In the north, innumerable small and large volcanoes dominate the landscape. Black, petrified lava streams cover the plains. One can see impressive rock formations and the deep fissurs of ravines and valleys like near Ndawe and Ngulia. Tsavo East is predominantly thorn bush savanna; the infamous Taru Desert borders on the park to the south. In former times there were extensive acacia forests. Long periods of drought and herds of elephants are the reasons for their disappearence.

Almost all types of animals indiginous to Kenya are represented in Tsavo National Park. The park has become world-famous for its "red elephants" whose colour is from the iron-rich laterit soil. With the end of the poaching of the 70's and early 80's, the number of elephants has increased again to about 10,000. Large herds assemble especially during the dry season at the Aruba Dam in Tsavo East as well as at Mudanda Rock and the water holes of the lodges. Hippopotamuses can

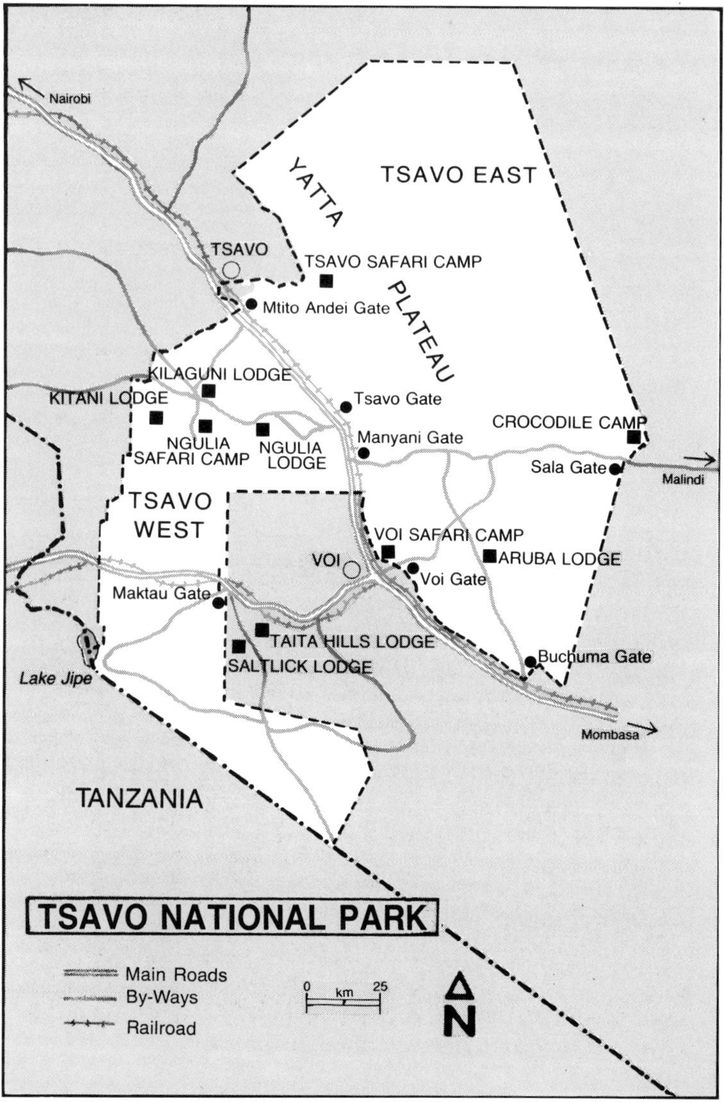
Nairobi
YATTA
TSAVO EAST
PLATEAU
TSAVO
TSAVO SAFARI CAMP
Mtito Andei Gate
KILAGUNI LODGE
KITANI LODGE
Tsavo Gate
CROCODILE CAMP
NGULIA SAFARI CAMP
NGULIA LODGE
Manyani Gate
Sala Gate
Malindi
TSAVO WEST
VOI SAFARI CAMP
ARUBA LODGE
VOI
Voi Gate
Maktau Gate
TAITA HILLS LODGE
SALTLICK LODGE
Buchuma Gate
Lake Jipe
Mombasa
TANZANIA
TSAVO NATIONAL PARK
Main Roads
By-Ways
Railroad
0 km 25
N

be observed best in Tsavo West near Mzima Springs, a lovely little spot. The most rhinoceroses of the country live in Tsavo, yet, because of the vast extensiveness of the park it is difficult to find them.

Tsavo National Park / **Practical Information**

Accomodation

Tsavo West:

Lake Jipe Safari Lodge, c/o P.O. Box 31097 Nairobi, Tel: 27623, £36.50/£58 ($68.50/$109).

Kilaguni Lodge, P.O. Box 2 Mtito Andei or c/o P.O. Box 30471 Nairobi, Tel: 336858, £40/£51.50 ($75/$97).

Ngulia Safari Lodge, c/o P.O. Box 30471 Nairobi, Tel: 336858, £36.50/£45 ($68.50/$84.50).

Taita Hills & Salt Lick Lodges, c/o P.O. Box 30624 Nairobi, Tel: 334000. Taita Hills: £49/£66.70 ($91.90/$125); Salt Lick: £56.50/£83 ($106/$156).

A "red giant" crosses the road in Tsavo National Park

Tsavo East:
Voi Safari Lodge, c/o P.O. Box 30471 Nairobi, Tel: 336858, £32/£43 ($60.50/$81). Self-catering camping areas are located at the Mtito Andei, Chyulu and Ziuani entrances in Tsavo West; in Tsavo East there are areas at the Voi entrance and the Aruba-Reservoir.

Vaccinations

At present, no vaccinations are required for visitors who fly to Kenya. However, confronted with the fact that the state of health of many people in some parts of the country is still rather precarious, and medical care is often insufficient, vaccinations for cholera and hepatitis are recommended. Furthermore, one should check into vaccination records: is there still sufficient protection against tetanus, typhoid fever and polio?

Vegetation

Since almost every type of climatic zone occurs in Kenya, it is not surprising that a large diversity of plant life is native to this country. Almost two thirds of the total area (the northern and eastern regions) is covered with deserts or semiarid regions of which the latter is a combination of savanna and sand and detritus fields with less than 500 mm (20 inches) of precipitation annually. Robust, fibrous **bunch grasses** eke out a meagre existence. Now and then, the monotony is broken by islands of dense bushlands and groups of **acacia trees.** Whenever the water table rises, the number of trees increases visibly. The most widely known tree, which cannot only be recognised by botanists, is the giant **baobab.** It stands in solitude and has the appearance of a tree because of its gnarled branches. Its roots, however, do not grow into the ground but upwards. Typical sights in the savanna are the **termite mounds,** which look similar to sand castles and approach a height 3 metres (around 10 feet). Armies of these insects numbering in the millions make sure that the sparse rainfall does not go unused. Their tunnels below the mounds, deep into the earth, loosen the soil and aerate the earth. Sometimes, these are even used as reservoirs of air and/or water by roots of trees. If the water table continues to rise, the **sausage tree** (so named because of its sausage-shaped fruit) and the **euphorbia trees** as well as the elegant **dum-palms** grow.
The visitor is confronted with a completely different scene at the coast. Regular precipitation allows for intensive agricultural utilisation of the 10 to 30 km (6 to 19 miles) wide coastal strip. Either private farms or cooperatives provide the basis for growing citrus fruits, cashews, corn (maize) and cotton as well as potatoes and

various types of beans. Extensive sisal and coconut plantations dominate the coast between Mombasa and Malindi. **Mangrove forests** which lie off the coast can best be seen from the Lamu archipelago. The seemingly impenetrable interior is a habitat for numerous species of birds.

Another fertile area is the region surrounding Lake Victoria in the country's western portion, where a quarter of the total population lives. Corn (maize) and rice is grown on the moist plains. Cassava, plantains (starchy bananas), millet and legumes are the basic foods in Kenya, grown in small gardens. Tea and coffee plantations were laid out by the white settlers in the highlands regions further inland.

The economic heart of Kenya is still the central highlands, bordered by its southern foothills, which stretch all the way to Nairobi and to the north by Mount Kenya. The western border of this region verges on Lake Victoria and Mount Elgon. In contrast to other equatorial regions in Africa, lofty mountain ranges like the Aberdare Mountains (reaching an altitude of 4,000 metres/13,080 feet), the Mau Escarpment and the continual settlement of this region for thousands of years have hindered the development of rain forests. Only the →*Kakamega Forest,* the last island of tropical rain forest in Kenya, is a reminder of the fact that Kenya is an equatorial region. All of the other forests, growing at altitudes of 1,500 to 2,500 metres (5,000 to 8,000 feet) have been cultivated with species of trees indigenous to Europe and North America. This was undertaken in order to halt the increasingly threatening advance of soil erosion in this heavily populated area. ''A tree for every child'' — this was a slogan presented by the president himself; however, this is only heeded half-heartedly: firewood is the only energy source for the rural population.

Visas →*Travel Documents*
Weather →*Climate, Tourist Season*

Wildlife

Kenya is Africa — this image has been developed by many beautiful films and books. At the present there are about 40 natural parks and game reserves. However, it may take quite a while before big game steps up in front of one's camera like in the movies. The reasons? Urbanisation and the steadily increasing population, and last but not least, the fact that it was legal well into the 1970's to hunt big game. This has reduced the wildlife population. Seventy years ago, the area of Nairobi (now a city with over a million residents) was the habitat for such a large number of animals, which can now only be found found in a few parks. The animals which have survived legal hunting are now hunted by groups of poachers. Although the Kenyan government prohibited hunting of endangered species and the export of furs and ivory, and despite the fact that the European Community banned the import of these goods, this could not prevent poaching. Underpaid park rangers and poachers (very often covered up by members of the government) battle it out in a bloody war with modern weapons. The result: rhinoceroses are almost extinct, and the number elephants has decreased so dramatically that the government is considering relocating elephants from Zimbabwe to Kenya.

In general, the visitors are not confronted with this East African tragedy during their short stay in Kenya. In fact, the national parks and game reserves were not established without reason. A memorable variety of species still characterises the wildlife of Kenya, even outside the parks. Regarding the visitors' general fear of poisonous spiders and snakes, one must say: yes, they exist. However, strangely enough, incidents involving these animals are almost never reported. The reason is that Kenya is not crawling with these and they try to flee as quickly as possible in a threatening situation.

A pair of cheetahs guard the spoils of their hunt

The animals of East Africa are well adapted to the extreme climatic conditions. Some of them can go without water for long periods and cover long distances during their migrations through the endless savanna, like the zebra (Kiswahili: punda milia) which lives in herds numbering a few hundred in most national parks. Often not far from their striped compatriates are the gnus (Kiswahili: nyumbu). Their flat, bearded heads and horse-like hindquarters are living proof that antelopes are not necessarily always elegant and graceful. This is especially true for the Thomson gazelles (Kiswahili: swala tomi). Their coat is yellow-brown, with black stripes at the sides with a radiantly white breast. The Grant gazelle (Kiswahili: swala granti) looks almost like the Thomson gazelle but is larger and does not have the "sporty" stripes. The impala (Kiswahili: swala pala) is also a wide-spread animal. It is heavier and more stable than the Grant gazelle. The males carry beautiful, lyre-shaped and twisted horns with a length of up to 70 cm (27 inches). The largest of all antelopes is the eland (Kiswahili: pofu) with a shoulder height of 180 cm (70 inches), weighing from 3 to 4 tons. Males and females have twisted antlers curved back, and even lions steer clear of these. Nevertheless, these are very shy animals, and it is rare that one will be able to take a picture of them. The smallest antelope is the dikdik — with a shoulder height of 30 cm (12 inches). Since they are only slightly larger than a rabbit, it is difficult to spot them. The most widely spread among the larger species of antelopes is the reed buck (Kiswahili: kuro). Its grey-brown coat is shaggy, the belly white, and only the males have twisted antlers curved back.

The bushlands are the favoured habitat for the giraffe (Kiswahili: twiga). Because of its height of over 5 metres (16½ feet), it is able to reach even the leaves on the higher branches. Different from other animals, it does not seek shade to shield it from the midday heat, but simply lies down, folding its legs gracefully beneath its body. Not particularly attractive, but the favourite of many visitors is the warthog (Kiswahili: ngiri). It lives on roots, which it digs out of the earth with powerful tusks. The warthog family sticks together, and when fleeing, the warthog will point its thin tail up like an antenna, often followed by tiny piglets in the same pose. The boar weighs more than 200 pounds and is a dangerous adversary for the big cats. The rhinoceros (Kiswahili: faru) will probably never win a beauty contest either. Meanwhile, it has also been added to the list of endangered species. One has to be very lucky to spot any of this primeval looking species in the →*Masai Mara Game Reserve* or at →*Nakuru National Park.* The most distinctive mark of this herbivore which weighs several tons is its mighty double-horn at the end of the muzzle. Because the Chinese still hold the superstitious belief that powder made from the rhinoceros horn can remedy potency problems, only a few number of these harmless giants could survive.

The most popular among the big cats is the lion (Kiswahili: simba) as can be observed time and again: while visitors can lose their interest in a zebra herd after only a few minutes, they can watch the prides of lions dozing in the midday heat until one of the cats sluggishly turns to the other side. Lions are not especially fond of chasing other animals for a long time. They either stalk their prey so closely that they can quickly pounce on it, or they work as a team, whereby most of the work is done by the female. A fully grown male lion weighs up to 400 pounds, and can reach a length of almost 3 metres (10 feet). The golden coat can hardly be distinguished from the dry grass of the savanna, so that it is difficult to spot the "king of the beasts" in the grass despite of its size. It is not easy to observe lions during the hunt. However, this is not the fault of the lions but of the safari agencies, who often conduct their safaris only until the early afternoon, while the lions favour the cool, late afternoon when hunting.

No less popular among the big cats is the cheetah (Kiswahili: duma). This highly specialised antelope hunter is able to run at a top speed of more than 120 km (75 miles) per hour — the fastest land mammal on earth — and certainly one of the most attractive. Its body is graceful, the legs are long and sinewy. When the cheetah is hunting, its tail operates like a balancing pole since it has to dart sideways when chasing its prey. The prey is not killed in a fight, but while it is fleeing it is pulled to the ground and it usually breaks its neck. Normally, cheetahs are very shy animals though they have become used to the visitors in the Mara and, especially, in →*Amboseli National Park.*

The hyena breaks other records. With its strong jawbones, it is even able to crush bones It can maintain a speed of 30 km (19 miles) per hour for several minutes. In contrast to the widely spread doctrine, hyenas are not purely scavengers, as lions are not purely hunters. An experiment has proven that lions are more likely to be attracted by the noise of the hyenas feeding on their prey than the other way around. Nor are the hyenas timid hunters as many people think. It takes quite a lot of courage to steal a meal from lions feeding on their prey. The jackal (Kiswahili: mbweha) is also both scavenger and hunter. Sometimes they even work together with the cheetahs, but since they do not have the weight to hold up against the cheetahs — they look like undernourished American coyotes. The jackals are usually left holding the bag when the prey is divvied up.

The birds of Kenya also has its superlatives. For example, the ostrich with a size of almost 3 metres (10 feet) is the largest bird of the world. It also lays the biggest eggs, weighing up to two pounds with a length of up to 15 cm (6 inches). The ostrich has given up flying for running a long time ago. It takes no effort for this bird to run at a speed of 60 km (38 miles) per hour! Just as striking as the ostrich is the marabou reaching a size of 180 cm (71 inches). It is a scavenger with a wingspan of more than 3 metres (about 10 feet inch). Its black and white plumage and the fleshy pouch on its bare neck give this bird the gloomy appearance of a grave digger. Marabous can be found at the water holes of the National Parks as well at Lake Nakuru, Baringo and Bogoria. The most spectacular sight within Kenyan bird life present the gigantic swarms of bright pink flamingos which have meanwhile become rare. The colour of their feathers is the result of the high carotene content in their food.

Where there are water holes that do not dry up, rivulets turn into rivers, and swamps to lakes, there are animals which are much more dependent on water than the savanna animals. This is very much the case with the hippopotamus (Kiswahili: kiboko). It spends its lazy day in the water, which bouyancy for its body weighing 1½ tons and maintains a low body temperature in the African heat. Only its eyes, nostrils and ears poke up out of the water. On land, the hippopotamus is faster than its short, stocky legs would imply. Though they are rather calm contemporaries, one be careful not accidentally block their escape route to the water. The African buffalo (Kiswahili: nyati) is native to the more moist regions. This vigorous animal with its deep-dark coat is very aggressive and is one of the most dangerous animals in the parks.

It spends the day within its herd in the shade of the trees and in the cool of the swamps. It becomes active only after nightfall. Like with the African buffalo one should keep some distance while observing the crocodile. Since it follows its instincts almost mechanically (more so than any other kind of animal) more people fall victim to it than to all big cats combined. The crocodile's teeth are made to tear their prey to pieces, not to chew. The crocodile, whose anatomy has remained unchanged for more than 60 million years, is cold-blooded. Therefore, they need to raise their body temperature by sunbathing.

There are many kinds of animals in the woodlands, too. One cannot fail to spot the elephants (Kiswahili: ndovu). In spite of the poaching in recent years, there are still large herds in the national parks. Though these pachyderms prefer staying in the protection of the forests can cover long distances during their migrations from waterhole to waterhole. They do not have any natural enemies, but because of their bad experience with the poachers, they are very cautious regarding visitors. Thus, it is advisable to keep some distance from herd of elephants. If they are irritated by a tourist looking for the best angle for a picture, these usually good-natured animals will convey their irritation by putting their ears forward and nervously stomping their front legs.

In comparison to the elephant, which lives in herds, the leopard (Kiswahili: chui) is an asocial animal. Being a confirmed single, it hunts on its own. Males and females only meet during the mating season. This spotted hunter, weighing up to 120 pounds, is only active by night and very shy — even park rangers have never seen them. During the daytime, one can only find traces of the leopard in the bushlands which hint at the animal's presence if one looks up the trees. Leopards are used to storing their prey — mostly antelopes — high up in the branches to protect it from greedy lions and hyenas. To carry the carcasses up into the branches is an exceptional feat of strength.

Far more obvious are the baboons. Among all of the of apes in Kenya, these are the most wide-spread. They live in troops of up to 50 animals, which are lead by the strongest males. The males are impressive, sometimes weighing up to 65 pounds with a size of more than 80 cm (31 inches). On campsites, these apes with a canine snout have become a plague threatening the food, the tents and the cars. Well-aimed stones are often a last resort to drive them away.

Youth Hostels →*Accomodation*